$ 10.95

PARK'S
SUCCESS WITH BULBS
(Including plants grown from Corms, Tubers, Rhizomes and Tuberous Roots)

PARK'S SUCCESS WITH BULBS

by
Alfred F. Scheider

In cooperation with the horticultural
staff of Geo. W. Park Seed Company, Inc.
under the direction of William J. Park
with
Photographs by the staff photographers
of the Geo. W. Park Seed Co., Inc.

GEO. W. PARK SEED CO., INC.
GREENWOOD, SOUTH CAROLINA

Contents

FOREWORD

The newest addition to our "Success" series has been produced by Alfred F. Scheider, aided by Park's horticultural team. We're extremely proud of this valuable addition to these publications. We feel it brings our customers and friends the latest and best information on growing the many plants normally started from bulbs, corms, roots and tubers. Al Scheider and the rest of the Park staff have done an outstanding job, and we feel that it will be a great service to horticulture.

Al Scheider, a native of New York, was educated at Cornell and has been involved for most of his life with the horticultural industry, heading Max Schling Seedsmen for nearly 20 years before coming to Park. Steeped in a lifelong love of plants and bulbs, he is eminently qualified to produce this work. Al is not only a very personable gentleman, but an extremely knowledgeable gardener and grower. We are pleased to have his background and expertise on our staff.

We hope this latest edition in our "Success" series will help you to be a better gardener. It has been another fun project for us.

William J. Park, President
Geo. W. Park Seed Co., Inc.
Greenwood, South Carolina

INTRODUCTION

When I was a little lad (as the old sea chanty goes), I started to learn about bulbs as part of a training or internship program to prepare me to enter the family horticultural business. I picked bulb orders (how I still remember the itch caused by counting out a thousand French Roman Hyacinths) and learned to recognize various bulb varieties by the color of their skins and shape of the bulb. Later, I made an arrangement with the pastor of the church next door, and was able to have a garden of my own. Hundreds of varieties of Narcissi, Tulips and Lilies grew in that New York City churchyard, and I was hooked! From then on, bulbous flowers have had a singular importance to me. As I worked in the business, under the tutelage of David Platt, a master plantsman, I began to learn the qualities that were considered in judging Narcissi and Amaryllis for show purposes, and my interest increased. It has never waned.

Imagine the delight and challenge I felt when Mr. William J. Park asked me to write a book on bulbs. And writing it has been challenging, but the difficulties have been eased by the splendid assistance I have received at every hand. And I feel an immense gratitude: to the librarians of the Horticultural Society of New York, and the New York and Brooklyn Botanic Gardens for their extraordinary helpfulness during a phase of my research; to the horticulturalists at Geo. W. Park Seed Co. for their enormous help in growing plants for this book and with the text itself; to photographers Allison Turner, David Brownlee, Bill Whitmore and John Elsley, whose efforts have resulted in many unique pictures to enhance this book; to Karen Park Jennings, for her splendid drawings; to David Brownlee for his invaluable help in layout and production; to Theresa Gooch, who labored long and arduously setting the type; to Viola Parrott, whose encouragement has lifted my flagging spirits on many occassions, and to William J. Park, for asking me to write it.

It is my hope that you will find this book to contain information that will help you to derive some of the same kind of pleasure from bulbous plants that I have enjoyed during my third of a century with them.

Alfred F. Scheider
Greenwood, South Carolina

Tulipa, Flower and Bulb

CHAPTER I

There's magic in bulbs! Those strange looking and often unprepossessing horticultural swellings give rise to some of the most striking and beautiful flowers in the plant kingdom . . . flowers to bring long-term loveliness to the garden, to be grown indoors to cheer the long winter days, and to provide a bounty of gorgeous cut flowers. Many of our most important flowers are grown from bulbs, and bulbous plants provide garden color from late winter to well after frost.

Nor is the contribution that bulbs make limited to ornamentals. Many of the world's most important food crops are derived from bulbous plants. The list is too numerous to mention here, but onions and their relatives, potatoes and sweet potatoes are just a few of the leading ones. In doing research in preparation for this book, we became aware of the impact of bulbous plants on the diet of the world, and also, that our western diet, considered so rich in variety, embraces only a small portion of the edibles of the world.

A list of the geographical sources of bulbs reads like a travelogue of the most exotic sort, for there is virtually no part of the world but has contributed its share of bulbous beauty. The route of Marco Polo is especially rich in its contributions, for vast numbers of species come from Asia Minor and the Orient. Africa has contributed enormously, with especially lavish legacies from the southern portion and many additions to our gardens from tropical and Mediterranean Africa. The Americas, too, both temperate and tropical portions, have been rich sources of bulbous materials.

Since the beginning of time, nomadic tribes have brought their native flora, much of it bulbous, with them in their migrations, spreading interesting plant materials to new lands. Soldiers billeted in foreign lands have often brought with them plants for medicine or food; thus the spread of the Madonna Lily *(L. candidum)* to western Europe and Great Britain is often attributed to Roman soldiers who made a salve for wounds from the bulbs. For hundreds of years, travellers to exotic places have returned to their homelands, bringing with them some of the bulbous bounty of the places they have visited, and introducing these exotic strangers to general culture. Diplomats, merchants and missionaries all have enriched horticulture in this way. While the fall of the Roman Empire and the Dark Ages saw a general diminution of interest in gardening, the crusades and the Renaissance sparked a revival in ornamental gardening activity. With the increase in travel for diplomatic and commercial purposes, and for exploration, more and more plants from foreign lands were introduced to the gardens of western Europe and Great Britain. Cortez described many of the plants of the New World, including the *Dahlia;* the Spanish introduced the potato *(Solanum tuberosum)* to North America, and Raleigh is reputed to have introduced it to Ireland. With the Dutch settlement in South Africa, the wealth of flora from that area, including *Oxalis, Freesia* and *Gladiolus,* spread to Europe. As interest in horticulture intensified, plant-gathering expeditions were mounted. The voyages of Captains Cook and Bligh were largely in this category. Plant hunters searched the New World, Africa and the Orient. Tournefort, Tradescant, Catesby, Bartram, Hartweg, Kaemfer, Thunberg and Siebold, to mention just a few, are immortalized in plant names. While many of the objects of their searches have remained horticultural curiosities, others have come to have great significance in the gardens of today.

Bulbs have long played a major economic role in world affairs. Egyptian scrolls from 1800 B. C. indicate the cultivation of Colchicums and Scillas for medicinal use. Anemones, Lilies and Narcissi also appear on tomb engravings. A thriving industry in Asia Minor, the Aegean, and later in England, revolved around the saffron trade, for saffron was important for medicines, dyestuff, perfumes and food flavorings. The fall-blooming Crocus, *C. sativus,* from whose stigmas saffron is derived, was first depicted on a Cretan jar circa 1500 B. C. It was described by Pliny the Elder as an important crop of Sicily (A. D. 1) and was later carried by the Romans to England, where Saffron Walden became the center of the dye industry. Today, while still grown for saffron in certain areas, it delights us with its cheerful lavender flowers in our October gardens. The story of the Tulip Madness in Holland in the 17th century, with speculation more frenzied than the wildest time in today's commodity market, and a final collapse far more extreme than

Colocasia esculentum

Hemerocallis

that of the Stock Market Collapse of 1929, needs no further telling. The failure of the potato crop in Ireland during the 1840's is a familiar story ... thus a simple tuber caused untold misery and loss of life, and resulted in a population migration that changed the face of history. Many of the bulbs we think of solely as ornamentals have been of tremendous economic significance in times past, or still are in ways not immediately obvious to the American gardener. *Camassia,* a native of temperate North America, which now adorns our spring gardens, served as a staple in the diet of several Indian tribes, particularly the Nez Perce, and bloody battles were fought for possession of the upland meadows where they grew so abundantly. The lush, tropical-appearing Elephant Ear, *Colocasia esculentum,* so valuable and striking as a background plant in today's summer gardens, is, as "taro", a major staple of diet for Polynesian peoples, as visitors to Hawaii who have eaten poi can attest. In plant breeding, the substance Colchicine is used to alter the genetic structure of plants by changing their chromosome count, thus giving rise to many exciting new tetraploid varieties. The same toxic material, in very dilute form (Wine of Colchicum), was long used as a specific treatment for gout. Colchicine is extracted from the corms of the fall-blooming *Colchicum autumnale,* which many grow as a garden bulb. Orris root, used in cosmetics and as a source of scent, is the ground-up rhizome of an *Iris.* The bulbs of many species of lilies, and such allies as *Cardiocrinum,* are still eaten today in considerable quantities by the people of Japan and China, as are the dried flowers and young rhizomes of *Hemerocallis.* Examples of the economic importance of bulbs are everywhere.

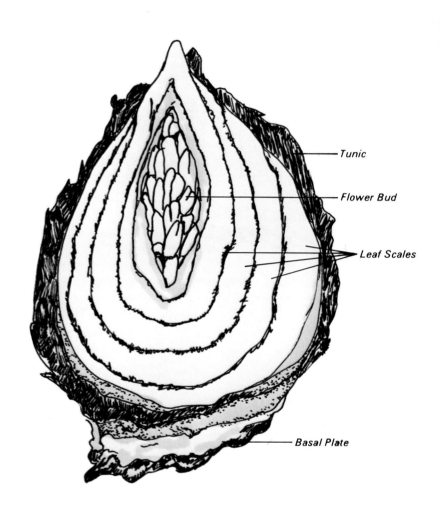

Tunic

Flower Bud

Leaf Scales

Basal Plate

The Structure of a Bulb

Imbricate Bulb (Lilium)   Tunicate Bulb (Tulipa)

What then is a bulb? Botanists define a true bulb as a usually subterranean modified leaf bud, consisting of a basal plate, short thick stem, and fleshy scales or leaf bases. It contains all the plant parts and serves as a storage organ. True bulbs are classified in two groups, those with a membrane or skin, known as "tunicate" (e. g. *Tulipa*), and those without the membrane and consisting of overlapping scales, known as "imbricate" (e. g. *Lilium*).

For the purpose of this book, we have included as "bulbous" plants those which do not grow from or produce true bulbs, but which are reproduced from somewhat similar storage organs and are often referred to as "bulbs" in garden practice. Such organs include corms, rhizomes, tubers and tuberous roots.

A corm is a solid, swollen part of a stem, usually subterranean, having a basal plate. It is completely expended at the end of the growing season and is replaced with new corms from buds on the side or top of the old one (e. g. *Gladiolus*).

A rhizome (or rootstock) is a usually horizontal stem on or under the ground that sends up a succession of leaves or stems at the apex (e. g. Bearded Iris).

A tuber is a short, thick, usually (but not always) subterranean stem or branch bearing buds or eyes and serving as a storage organ (e. g. *Begonia x tuberhybrida*).

A tuberous root is a swollen, food storing root with eyes located, not on the root itself, but on the base of the stem (e. g. *Dahlia*).

While all of the above have precise botanical meanings, in everyday gardening the distinctions are often obscured, and the term "bulb" is commonly applied to all of them. In the encyclopedic portion of this book we have indicated the actual class of reproductive organ. All of the groups in question are highly developed food storage mechanisms

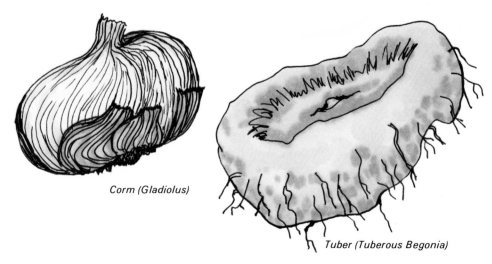

Corm (Gladiolus)

Tuber (Tuberous Begonia)

which enable the plant to survive underground, often in areas that have long seasons that are not conducive to active growth. If you were to examine the geographical origins of many of the hardy, spring blooming bulbs, for example, you would find that many come from areas with a "continental climate", where a beneficent spring growing season is followed by a hot, dry summer, unsuitable for plant growth, and in turn, followed by a severe winter. Many of the summer flowering bulbs, on the other hand, are products of areas that enjoy moist, gentle summers and falls.

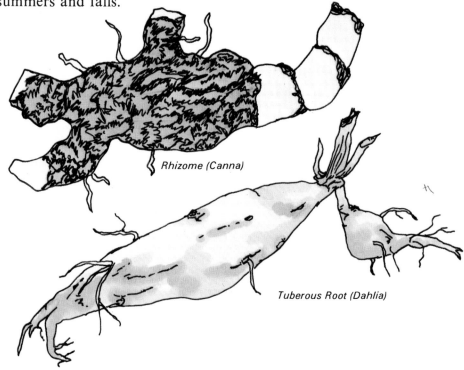

Rhizome (Canna)

Tuberous Root (Dahlia)

CHAPTER II
PLANTING BULBS

Guidelines to Buying Bulbs

You have decided that you want to plant some bulbs this fall. How then do you best go about obtaining them?

In today's marketing structure, bulbs are available from four source categories: 1. mail order horticultural firms, who publish extensive catalogs of their bulb offerings, 2. promotional mail order firms, who usually offer one sort of bulb, or at best a very limited choice, 3. garden shops, who display bulbs for sale, 4. mass merchandizers, such as supermarkets, who often offer packaged bulbs.

When you buy a bulb, you buy a promise of future beauty. You can examine it for general soundness, but you cannot test-drive it as you would a car, nor try its edge as you would a knife. To a great extent, then, you are buying "blind". Your greatest protection is in the character of the purveyor . . . his reputation, concern and knowledge of bulbs, and the importance of bulbs to him in his overall operation. Category 4, the mass-marketers, may be sincere and honest, but bulbs are a minor item of inventory for them. Their expertise in the field is limited, and the selection they offer is almost always prepackaged, limited and usually confined to mixtures. Moreover, the conditions under which they distribute and display their bulb inventory is rarely conducive to keeping the bulbs at their best. Those in Category 2, the promotional bulb sellers, tend to offer, "at unbelievably low prices", bulbs that will grow without care, produce hundreds of long-lasting flowers of incredible beauty, and, no doubt, play a tune as they grow! Such offers are to be taken, not with a grain, but rather with a whole pound of salt!

There remain, categories 1 and 3. The latter offers the advantages of visual inspection, and usually knowledgeability and helpful advice. You also have the advantage of immediate availability. Weighed against this are the disadvantages of storage under conditions usually unfavorable for the health of the bulb. Bulbs are, after all, living plants, even if in a dormant stage. When you order from a mail order horticultural catalog house, while you will have to wait a few days for your order to arrive, the advantages of a wider selection that has been kept under ideal storage conditions may far outweigh the few days' wait.

What should you order? This is largely a matter of the location in which the bulbs will be planted, the purpose for which you are planting, and, above all, personal preference. Obviously, if you can provide only shaded locations, you would be ill-advised to order bulbs that require full sun. The converse is also true. Catalog descriptions, or the advice of your garden center, can provide many helpful hints, but always order the best available! The initial cost of your bulb purchase is insignificant, compared to the rewards of years of performance that top-quality bulbs will provide.

Mixtures

Bulb mixtures are a popular way of buying quality bulbs at a somewhat reduced price. If you are planting bulbs primarily to use as cut flowers, mixtures are splendid. If, however, you are planning to use mixtures for naturalizing, a widespread usage, think again. Rarely do flowers grow naturally in mixed colors! Since naturalizing means attempting to reproduce that which is found in Nature, we feel that it is far more effective to buy individual varieties and plant them in clumps of one variety, one blending into the next. Try it!

When To Plant

Most hardy bulbs become available in late August or early September. Planting from then until the end of November usually produces the best results. Fall-bloomers are obviously planted somewhat earlier. Some of the spring-flowering hardy bulbs respond best to early planting—information to this effect is included in the encyclopedic section under the genus in question. By and large, towards the southern limit of their range, early planting should be avoided, lest undesired premature growth occurs. Spring planted, tender bulbs are planted when soil and air temperatures are sufficiently warm for them to begin almost immediate growth.

Soil Preparation

In planting bulbs, drainage is of prime importance. While a bulb may survive a year of poor drainage and flower the first spring, it is unlikely that it will establish or colonize under such adverse conditions; it is more apt to give up the ghost. Many of the hardy bulbs lend themselves to planting on slopes, where drainage is especially good, in raised beds, or if elsewhere, in soils whose drainage is either naturally good or has been improved through the liberal incorporation of sharp sand and/or compost. For the true bulbs, fertility is of lesser consideration, since many of the areas to which the bulbs are native have poor or infertile soils. One of the most frequently recommended fertilizers for bulbs is bonemeal, which is slow-acting and mild. Well-decomposed organic matter of vegetable origin will improve the soil texture, but the caution to avoid animal manures (assuming that such were readily available in today's world) is a good one, since the use of such tends to promote fungus and bacterial diseases.

Surface	• Begonia • Eucharis • Haemanthus • Hippeastrum • Vallota • Veltheimia	Surface
½ in.	• Achimenes	½ in.
1 in.	• Caladium • Paeonia • Sinningia	1 in.
1½ in.	• Canna • Ranunculus	1½ in.
2 in.	• Calochortus • Eucomis • Mertensia • Freesia • Oxalis • Panax • Incarvillea • Iphion • Crocus	2 in.
2½ in.	• Anemone • Eranthus • Galanthus • Ornithogalum • Sparaxis • Puschkinia • Scilla • Solanum	2½ in.
3 in.	• Chionodoxa • Fritillaria (Melcagris) • Polianthes • Ixia • Ixiolirion • Milla • Muscari	3 in.
3½ in.	• Acidanthera • Camassia • Colchicum • Endymion • Lewisia • Leucojum • Zantedeschia • Spreklia	3½ in.
4 in.	• Bletilla • Brodiaea • Colocasia • Hymenocallis • Lycoris • Tigridia • Watsonia	4 in.
4½ in.	• Gloriosa • Nerine	4½ in.
5 in.	• Sternbergia	5 in.
5½ in.	• Eucomis	5½ in.
6 in.	• Dahlia • Dracunculus • Eremurus • Fritillaria • Imperialis • Gladiolus • Narcissus	6 in.
7 in.	• Tulipa	7 in.
8 in.	• Lilium	8 in.

Depth of Planting Chart

When You Have Your Bulbs

It would be nice to have completed all your soil preparation before your bulbs arrive. If you haven't, or if demands on your time prevent immediate planting, open the packages to permit some air circulation, and store out of the sun in a cool location such as a garage or cellar.

Depth and Spacing

As a rule of thumb, plant true bulbs and corms so that they are covered to a depth of three times their maximum diameter. This will vary with soil types; in light soils, planting deeper yet may produce additional years of flowering, particularly in the case of Tulips. In heavier soils that have not been rectified, it may be necessary to set the bulbs more shallowly than the 3-times rule. Exceptions also occur with certain species, determined by their specific growth peculiarities. These are stated in the encyclopedic portion of this book. In planting formal beds, as of Tulips or Hyacinths, a more even effect can be achieved by removing the soil to the desired depth, setting the bulbs, and then covering them with soil. Blooming heights and spacing will be more uniform.

There are no hard-and-fast rules for spacing bulbs. In general, we have observed that most gardeners tend to plant too few and space them too far apart. Whether or not this is a function of their cost we do not know, but in the garden, the best effect is achieved through planting small groups of a variety, closely massed. This is particularly true of the minor bulbs . . . *Muscari, Chionodoxa, Crocus, Scilla* and the like, whose charming effect to a great extent depends on their use in mass. Bulbs are more appealing in groups of individual varieties or species, rather than in mixtures. Naturalizing, or the planting of bulbs so that they appear to be in situ, instead of in formal arrangements, is a very effective way of employing *Narcissus, Galanthus, Eranthis,* and *Endymion,* to name just a few. To get them to appear as if they grew there naturally, rather than having been planted by the hand of man, requires a good deal of artfulness. Some authors recommend that a handful of bulbs be thrown about, then planted where they fall. We prefer to pick our site for maximum eye-appeal, plant irregular groups of the bulbs in question where they will give the best visual effect, allowing the group to thin out at the edges, and possibly merge with another group of a different sort. When naturalizing, space somewhat further apart than normal to allow for natural increase without the necessity of digging the bulbs up in a few years to divide and replant.

Care When Blooming

Bulbs require little care when actually in bloom. Some, Tulips in particular, will benefit from a modest application of fertilizer at that time. This seems to promote flower production for the following year (sewage sludge is what the professional bulb growers use). If picking flowers, try to remove as little foliage as possible.

After Care

Bulb foliage continues to perform its function in photosynthesis after flowering has ended. Do not remove foliage until it has yellowed completely, since it continues to manufacture food to keep the plant alive and build next year's flowers. This may tend to offend the compulsively neat, particularly when bulbs are used in formal beds, but by overplanting your bulbs with early-blooming annuals, the yellowing foliage can effectively be hidden. In naturalized situations, there is no such problem. While foliage should not be removed while it is still functional, spent flowers should be removed to prevent the plant from setting seed, since this process is highly energy-consuming and may inhibit future flowering. Spent foliage, when removed, should be destroyed, not added to the compost pile.

Many bulbs can be left undisturbed for years, but occasionally will have multiplied to the extent that they become overcrowded and flower production declines. This happens frequently with old *Narcissus* plantings. When scanty spring bloom indicates that this is the case, bulbs should be allowed to ripen their foliage, then dug in late summer, divided and replanted to allow room for future increase.

CHAPTER III
FORCING

"Forcing" is the process of growing a plant, (for the purpose of this discussion, a bulb), under artifical indoor conditions so that we may enjoy its flower or ornamental foliage indoors at a time when it would not otherwise be productive. This has been done for hundreds of years. Almost everyone has had some experience of bulb forcing; the Paperwhite Narcissi that you grew as a child in pebbles and water are a prime example.

As far as cultural requirements are concerned, we may conveniently divide bulbs for forcing into 3 groups: those from tropical or subtropical climates, which will grow happily at normal household temperatures; hardy bulbs which in nature grow in areas exposed to freezing or near-freezing temperatures and require a period of such low temperature to break their dormancy or rest-period before they will initiate growth; and the so-called "Cape Bulbs", coming from South Africa or other places of similar climate, most of which require cool night temperatures (50° F.) to flower satisfactorily. While all three groups can be forced successfully, it is obviously the first group that is the easiest to handle in the average home. The limiting factor for the Cape Bulbs is excessively high night temperature common to most dwellings. The hardy group is limited by the absence of near freezing temperatures, combined with higher temperatures than optimum, both day and night. The beginner would be well advised to concentrate his efforts to the first group, gradually experimenting with the others as he acquires experience. A greenhouse or sun porch, maintained at low temperatures, will greatly enhance the chances of success with the other two groups.

Pots

In general, pots for bulb forcing are shallower than those used for other plants. They may be of clay or plastic. The former dry out more quickly, so watering practices must be adjusted to the kind of pot used. In either case the pot should have drainage holes. Containers without such provision for drainage should be avoided, save with a very few bulbs whose requirements are more forgiving.

Tuberous Begonia Kit   *Narcissus Kit*

Potting Media

True bulbs contain within themselves all the parts of the plant and flower. For many of them, the medium exists merely to provide proper moisture and a degree of support. Corms, rhizomes, tubers and tuberous roots are not so constructed, and the medium must also provide a greater degree of nourishment so that the plant can develop and flower. Growing media may be potting soils, composed of garden loam, sharp sand and organic matter, in various proportions. Or the newer soilless mixtures may be used, based on peat moss with the addition of perlite and other inert materials, primarily included to make the mixture more porous. Because of the convenience, wider availability and sterile qualities of the various soilless mixtures, there has been a great tendency in recent years in their direction. Since these mixtures are basically without nutrients, the latter must be provided as the culture of the individual specimen requires. This is easily accomplished, either through watering with soluble plant foods or through the use of pelleted, slow-release fertilizers, the latter being the more commonly used method.

Potting

Depth of planting will vary from type to type. Generally, for forcing purposes, the bulbs need be barely covered, while some kinds are best planted with a portion of the bulb exposed. Directions for the various genera appear in the encyclopedic portion of this book.

Watering

After you have potted your forcing bulbs, they should be watered thoroughly. (If you have used a soilless mix, it should have been wetted before use, since peat-based materials tend to reject water when dry). Subsequent watering will depend on the genus and are covered in the encyclopedic section, but in general, bulbs should be kept barely moist until growth is evident, after which watering should be increased. The question, "How often should I water my . . . ?" is unanswerable, except

Scilla Kit

Hippeastrum (Amaryllis) Kit

to say, "When it needs it". This is a function of experience and knowing the moisture requirements of the plant in question. Generally speaking, bulbs in clay pots require more frequent watering than do those in plastic; those in soil need more frequent watering than those in soilless mixtures. Weight of pot, color of medium, and condition of plant will provide guidelines.

Fertilizers

In general, bulbs require little in the way of fertilizer to bloom satisfactorily the first year. Those to be grown on for subsequent years will require some, as will those other bulb relatives that are not true bulbs. As with watering, too much is worse than too little; if in doubt, don't!

Light

All plants require light, even those that we say perform well in shade. The exact amount of light will vary with the species. Light can be natural sunlight or can be provided by one of the many good plant-growing light structures available to the public. The plant's stage of growth often affects the amount of light required. You will find that by fitting your selection of plant materials to the kind and intensity of light you can provide, your results will markedly improve.

Temperatures

As we mentioned in the beginning of this chapter, temperature is often the limiting factor in success with certain kinds of bulbs. We all tend to keep our homes too warm, and despite astronomical heating costs, will probably continue to do so. Excessively high night temperatures are particularly limiting. Most plants prefer a 7° to 10° F. drop in temperature from day to night, and many bulbs will not flower if night temperatures exceed 50° F. Learn which ones they are, and unless you can provide the cool temperatures they require, grow others, at least at first. Specific temperature requirements are set forth in the encyclopedic portion of this book.

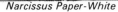
Narcissus Paper-White   Narcissus Cragford

Drainage

One of the most universal requirements for bulbs is good drainage. Take care that pots do not become waterlogged or bulbs will rot.

Pests

Fortunately, if you buy good bulbs and use a sterile medium, pests are not a major problem.

Convallaria

CHAPTER IV
THE BULB INDUSTRY

The Bulb Industry

Commercial bulb growing is almost as old as recorded history. We have spoken elsewhere of the scrolls and tomb drawings of ancient Egypt, which depicted such bulbs as *Colchicum* and *Scilla* being cultivated for medicinal purposes, and talked of the thriving trade in saffron, derived from *Crocus sativus,* which involved whole areas of the Aegean and eastern Mediterranean.

Bulb production for ornamental or garden purposes probably began in the Thirteenth Century in Asia Minor. Certain it is that the Tulips that de Busbeq found in such lavish abundance in Turkey, during the middle of the Sixteenth Century, were not wild species, but rather the product of quite sophisticated hybridization, carried on by a bulb industry, albeit probably an amateur one. The introduction of Tulips to western Europe, and subsequently to Holland, marked the beginning of an industry that was to achieve almost legendary proportions. From small beginnings toward the end of the Seventeenth Century, the business grew, first modestly during the Eighteenth Century, and then with amazing rapidity during the latter half of the Nineteenth.

Nor was commercial bulb production limited to Holland. Hyacinths, after their introduction to Europe through Italy, were grown and hybridized on a large scale in France and later produced in great quantities in Germany. A substantial bulb industry arose and still continues in Great Britain, largely in Lincolnshire, but also around Norfolk and in Cornwall. Totalling about 10,000 acres, it produces Tulips, Daffodils, Snowdrops and other minor bulbs, as well as *Iris* and *Gladiolus,* the last primarily for the cut flower market. Certain Narcissi, particularly Tazetta types, are grown in the Channel Islands.

But when one thinks of bulbs, one tends to think of Holland. That one small nation could so dominate an industry is truly remarkable, particularly when one considers that bulb productions is concentrated in two small areas, which formerly embraced only about 20,000 acres, divided between two areas. As land has come into ever-increasing demand for housing and industrial use, this acreage has decreased, but mechanized methods have permitted more intensive production; thus more bulbs are produced. on less land.

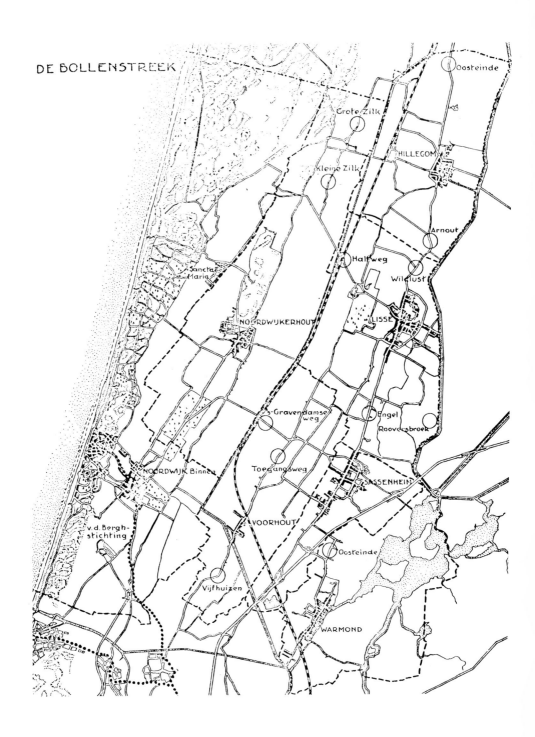

DE BOLLENSTREEK

The most famous area for bulb production in Holland is known as the Bollenstreeck. It consists of about 25 square miles, starting at Haarlem, running westward to the coast at Zandvoort, south through Noordwijk to the Hague and along the main Amsterdam road to Sassenheim, then back to Haarlem along the Sassenheim-Haarlem road. It grows slightly less than 50% of the nation's crop, but is the area most famed and most visited for bulbs. The other area starts at the mouth of the Amsterdam canal, runs to Bergen, just west of Alkmaar, thence diagonally to Medemblik, then southeast to Enkhuizenn and back to Bererwijk and Ijmuiden.

What determines where bulbs are grown? First of all, historical continuity; i.e., if bulbs have been a commercial crop in an area, they tend to continue to be as long as the economics of production remain favorable. Soil and climatic conditions must be right for the crop in question . . . not necessarily sandy as it is in Holland, for bulbs have successfully been produced on silty or volcanic soils . . . and terrain must favor bulb production. Soil drainage must be good and temperatures favorable. Above all, land prices must be low enough to permit the land to continue to be used for agricultural purposes. In recent years, as land prices have risen in Holland, the land devoted to bulb growing has been shrinking, and production has been concentrated on those varieties which enjoy the highest demand and are the most economical to produce. Thus the trade, despite ongoing hybridization, tends to produce many fewer total varieties than were available even a generation ago. This is dictated by economic considerations.

The word "bulb" immediately conjures up images of Holland, but, although bulb production probably ranks much more important there in terms of gross national product, Holland is by no means the only major producer of bulbs. From Belgium come Tuberous-rooted Begonias, *Sinningia* (Gloxinia) and *Clivia;* England and Ireland produce *Narcissus* in great number, and the former also large quantities of *Iris, Gladiolus* and *Galanthus,* as well as some splendid Tuberous Begonias; France is known for *Lilium candidum, Narcissus Tazetta* and *Tulipa Clusiana;* Germany provides *Achimenes;* from India come *Achimenes, Eucharis, Lycoris* and *Zephyranthes;* Israel is increasingly producing *Narcissus Tazetta,* plus *Anemone, Ranunculus* and *Dahlia;* Japan, once preeminent in the production of *Lilium,* still produces quantities, in addition to *Hippeastrum, Lycoris* and *Pecteilis; Hippeastrum* are also extensively produced in South Africa. The United States and Canada play a major role in commercial bulb production: Oregon probably produces 75% of the world's Lilies; Tuberous Begonias are grown in huge quantities in California, as are *Anemones* and *Ranunculus.* The Pacific Northwest boasts an important *Narcissus*-growing industry, and grows quantities of bulbous *Iris.* Florida grows large quantities of *Caladiums,* as well as Callas, *Colocasia, Oxalis,* Tuberoses and *Gloriosa. Gladiolus* and Dahlias are grown in quantity in many areas of the United States, wherever land prices permit and persons interested in their culture may be found.

Increasingly, modern technology is being applied to the commercial bulb-farming business, decreasing the amount of hand labor required and increasing productivity per acre. But, in the case of a few rarities, the only sources are a few "Poppa and Mama" growers or collectors who obtain bulbs from the wild state.

So, you will see, just as the bulbs that you enjoy in your garden or home are native to many parts of the world, so too is their production achieved in diverse areas.

CHAPTER V
THE BULBS

Achimenes   Acidanthera

Achimenes hybrids   MAGIC FLOWER   Rhizome
Gesneriaceae, Tropical America   Zone 10

USES: Pot Plant, Window Boxes, Hanging Baskets

HABIT: Tender perennials, many of trailing or pendulous habit, growing 12-24 inches and bearing rather hairy leaves and tubular flowers in a wide range of color. Flowers are abundantly produced during late spring, summer and fall. The breeding of the hybrid form now on the market is quite confused and derives, in part from such species as: *A. antirrhina,* with leaves reddish beneath and yellow flowers marked with red or purple; *A. erecta* with leaves red or red-veined and red or rose blossoms; *A. flava* with yellow flowers spotted with red; *A. grandiflora,* with leaves often red below and red-violet flowers; *A. heterophylla,* with bright orange-red or scarlet blossoms; *A. longiflorum,* with leaves red below and lilac, purple or white flowers; *A. mexicana,* with purple or blue flowers; and *A. pedunculata* with orange-red blooms.

CULTURE: From January on, using an acid, light potting soil or peat-based potting medium, plant the pinecone-like rhizomes at a depth of ½-1 inch, setting 4-6 to a six-inch pot or hanging basket. Place in a warm situation (above 60° F.), in filtered sun or partial shade, and keep moist. A slow-release fertilizer may be applied to the medium at planting time, or you can feed after bud formation with a soluble plant food. When plants die back in fall, remove the rhizomes, which will have increased tremendously in number, from the growing medium and store dry at 65-70° F. until time to replant.

Acidanthera Murieliae   ABYSSINIAN SWORD LILY   Corm
Iridaceae, Ethiopia   Zone 10

USES: Garden, Cut Flowers

HABIT: Plants with Gladiolus-like foliage and fragrant white flowers, marked with maroon in the center. Flowers are borne in late summer on 12-24 inch plants.

CULTURE: Plant in full sun in a well-drained, gritty soil to which ample leaf mold, compost, or well-decayed manure has been added. Set corms 3-4 inches deep and 6 inches apart, and keep amply watered until blooming finishes. After blooms are finished, allow to dry. Successive plantings, 2-3 weeks apart, will provide a longer blooming period. After foliage has died down, lift, discard old corm, keeping new one and storing dry at 70° F. until next planting season.

Acorus

Agapanthus

Acorus   SWEET FLAG   Rhizome
Araceae, Asia   Zone 5

USES: Bog Gardens, Waterside Plantings

HABIT: Rush-like plants for marshy places. The flowers, typical of the family, are of little landscape value; it is the leaves for which *Acorus* is grown. *A. Calamus* grows to about 4 feet in height and the foliage has a pleasant cinnamon fragrance. A variegated form provides excellent foliage contrast. *A. gramineus,* a dwarfer species with narrower leaves, is also found in a variegated type with dark green and cream leaves.

CULTURE: Plant about 1 foot apart in moist, boggy soil in sun or partial shade. The smaller species can also be grown in the garden, provided that the soil is constantly moist.

NOTE: An extract of the root is used in pharmacology. In olden days, the leaves were strewn on the floor to add a pleasant scent to otherwise malodorous homes.

Agapanthus orientalis   LILY-OF-THE-NILE (BLUE)   Rhizome
Amaryllidaceae, South Africa   Zone 9

USES: Garden, Containers and Tubs, Patio Planters

HABIT: Summer blooming plants to 2 feet in height with strap-shaped, evergreen leaves and umbels of tubular or bell-shaped flowers in shades of blue and white. The variety *'Mooreanus'* is somewhat hardier than the species and will survive outdoors with protection to Zone 6.

CULTURE: Although hardy in Zones 9-10, *Agapanthus* grows best when potbound, hence is best grown, even where hardy, in tubs. Plant with the roots just covered, in large tubs filled with a porous potting medium to which powdered limestone has been added. Set in sun or light shade (the warmer the region, the more desirable is some shade), and supply ample moisture during the active growing season. Feed monthly. After blooming, discontinue fertilizer applications and markedly reduce watering. In areas north of Zone 9, bring containers indoors before danger of frost, or grow as house plants year round.

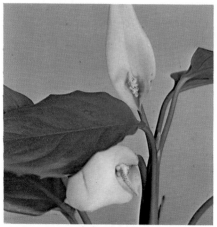

Aglaonema

Allium unifolium

Aglaonema species　　CHINESE EVERGREEN　　　　Rhizome
Araceae, Tropical Asia

USES: Pots

HABIT: Lush plants with stout canes and ovate or lanceolate leaves in green, with or without contrasting markings. The rather inconspicuous, typically aroid flowers have greenish-yellow spathes, followed by red berries. *A. brevispathum* has narrow leaves of medium green, sometimes with white markings; *A. commutatum* comes in a wide range of forms with variegated leaves in a number of color patterns, while the most widely grown of all, *A. modestum,* is an unmarked rich green.

CULTURE: Easily adaptable to water culture, and often grown as a house plant in this way. One of the most indestructible of house plant subjects, flourishing under warm conditions, even with very low light intensities. If grown in soil, the latter should be retentive and kept moist, and plants are best grown with some filtered light.

Allium Ornamental Species　　　　　　　　　　Bulb
Amaryllidaceae, Northern Hemsiphere　　　　　Various

USES: Garden, Rock Garden, Pots, Dried Arrangements

HABIT: Ornamental plants, from 6-60 inches in height, related to the onion and with foliage often onion-scented when crushed. Umbels of flowers, in a wide range of colors, and often delightfully fragrant, are produced variously from spring to fall. *A. giganteum,* with huge, 9 inch umbels of violet-purple flowers borne on 4 foot plants during July, is a spectacular plant for the back of the border; while shorter species, including *A. aflatunense,* lilac flowers on 2½-5 foot plants in May and June; *A. caeruleum,* cornflower blue flowers in July on 2½ foot plants; *A. Moly,* bright yellow flowers in June on 1½ foot plants; *A. neapolitanum,* fragrant white flowers in May and June on 18 inch plants; *A. karataviense, white flowers shaded rosy violet in May and June on 6-10 inch plants; A. sphaerocephalum,* red flowers on 2 foot plants; and *A. unifolium,* pink flowers on 24 inch stems, are suitable for the border or rock garden. Many of the smaller species are also excellent for forcing in pots.

CULTURE: Outdoors, plant bulbs in a sunny, well-drained location at a depth equal to their maximum axis. Feed during the growing season. Tender varieties should be lifted in the fall and stored at 70° F. Many of the smaller species are excellent for house or greenhouse culture in pots. Set in well-drained potting medium and grow in a cool, sunny location, providing ample water during active growth.

Garlic

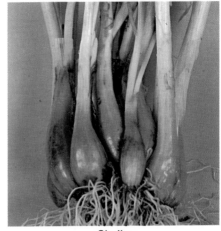

Shallot

Allium, Edible species   Bulb
Amaryllidaceae, Northern Hemisphere   Zone 4

USES: Vegetable, Flavoring

HABIT: *Allium Cepa,* Onion, is among the oldest of cultivated edibles, appearing in artwork on ancient Egyptian tombs. Its actual geographical origin is uncertain, but probably lies somewhere between the Caspian Sea and China. In addition to the *Cepa* Group which includes those with single bulbs and no bulbils, there is the Proliferum group which includes Egyptian Tree Onions, which produce bulbils but no seeds, and the Aggregatum Group, which includes Multiplier Onions and Shallots, with multiple bulbs. This is the most important species, economically. Next in importance is *Allium sativum* (Garlic). It produces bulbs divided into several cloves, and grows to 2 feet with white or pinkish flowers. *A. Schoenoprasum,* Chives, does not produce well-defined bulbs, and is grown for its cylindrical leaves which are used in flavoring and as a garnish. The plants, with rose-pink flowers, are also extremely attractive in the garden. *A. Scorodoprasum,* Giant Garlic, has larger bulbs with a somewhat less pungent nature than *A. sativum.* *A. tuberosum,* Chinese Chives, has, unlike *A. Schoenoprasum,* conspicuous bulbs, but is grown for the foliage. The leek, *A. Ampeloprasum,* has bulbs that are very poorly defined, but is grown for the lower portion of the stem, which is used blanched as a vegetable. *A. fistulosum,* the so-called Japanese or Welsh Bunching Onion, lacks well-defined bulbs, and is used as a "green onion" of extremely mild flavor. *A. chinense,* the Rakkyo of Japan, looks like Chives when growing, but has well-developed bulbs. It is dormant in summer and flowers in the fall.

CULTURE: Onions are frequently grown on muck soils, although they will succeed on mineral ones as well. They may be started from seeds, sets (small bulbs), or started transplants. Seed will produce relatively small bulbs the first year; the other two methods produce larger ones. Onions are biennial, and are highly reactive to day-length, so varieties for northern and southern culture are different. Chives, Chinese Chives and Welsh Bunching Onions are most frequently started as seeds, while Garlic, Giant Garlic and Shallots are usually from "cloves" or bulb divisions. Leeks are grown from seed, and as they grow, should be hilled up to extend the white edible portion of the top growth. All profit from a highly fertile soil, full sun and ample moisture.

Alocasia

Alstroemeria

Alocasia species and hybrids　　ELEPHANT EAR　　　　Rhizome
Araceae, Tropical Asia

USES: Containers

HABIT: Lush plants have large, often lobed fleshy leaves, frequently colored and highly ornamental. The flowers are of little ornamental value. *A. cucullata* (Chinese Ape), has large, lobed leaves of bright, glossy green. The roots are sometimes eaten in the Orient. *A. cuprea* (Giant Caladium), has 10-12 inch leaves with dark green blades and purple undersides. *A. plumbea* has arrow-head shaped leaves, olive-green flushed purple above, reddish purple below; *A. Sanderana* has narrow triangular gleaming silver-green leaves marked and margined in white and purple beneath; *A. Watsoniana* has corrugated blue green leaves, prominently veined in white with a red-purple lower surface. *A. x amazonica* has dark green foliage with the scalloped edges and veins white and standing out vividly against the dark background.

CULTURE: Requires high temperatures and high humidity. Best grown potted in sphagnum moss which is kept constantly moist in a warm (70° F.), shaded location. During the winter months, the temperature can be reduced to 60° F. or so, and moisture levels somewhat lowered.

Alstroemeria species　　PERUVIAN LILY,　　　　Tuberous Root
　　　　　　　　　　　　　　LILY-OF-THE-INCAS
Alstroemeriaceae, South America　　　　　　　　　　Zone 7

USES: Garden, Pots, Cutting

HABIT: 1½-4 foot plants bearing clusters of fragrant flowers in bright colors, often with contrasting markings. In addition to the species mentioned here, there are numerous varieties and hybrids commonly grown: *A. aurantiaca,* probably the hardiest, has flowers of orange or yellow, spotted with red. *A. Pelegrina,* lavender flowers spotted with red-purple, *A. pulchra (chilensis)* has blooms of white or pink, marked with yellow, red or purple. All bloom in midsummer in the garden.

CULTURE: In the garden, plant in spring in sun or light shade in a well-drained location. A moist, sandy loam to which an ample supply of humus has been added is best. Set roots 6-9 inches deep and 12 inches apart. Feed during growing season. North of Zone 7, dig in fall and store roots cool in moist sand. Zone 7 and south, roots can be left in the ground over winter, using winter mulch.

To grow in pots, plant in fall and water sparingly until growth starts, thereafter more liberally. Dry off gradually after blooming.

NOTE: Alstroemerias are of some commercial importance as a florist's cut-flower.

Amomum

Amorphophallus

Amomum compactum   CARDAMOM GINGER   Rhizome
Zingiberaceae, East Indies   Zone 10

USES: Pots, Containers

HABIT: Plants usually growing to about 3 feet in height (taller in the wild), with glossy green leaves, up to 10 inches long and 3 inches across. The roots and leaves are aromatic when rubbed or crushed. The tubular flowers are yellow, marked with purple. The aromatic seeds from this plant are sometimes used as a substitute for the true cardamom, *Elettaria Cardamomum.*

CULTURE: Grow in a partially shaded location, using a highly fertile potting mixture and providing a constant supply of moisture. Normal household night temperatures will suit it well.

Amorphophallus Rivieri   DEVIL'S TONGUE   Corm
Araceae, Southeast Asia   Zone 10

USES: Pots. Widely grown in Orient for its edible corms.

HABIT: Large plants with tripartite, umbrella-like, serrated leaves, borne atop a 3-4 foot mottled stem, and appearing after the plants flower. Large calla-lily-like spathe, 1-3 feet long, green spotted and shading to purple at the edge, is adorned with a dark red, 1-3 foot spadix. Flowers emit a carrion odor.

CULTURE: Pot in a compost-rich mixture and water sparingly until growth starts. Grow under conditions of filtered light. Increase watering as plant begins active growth and fertilize periodically; then, after foliage dies back, withhold water, lift corm and store cool over winter.

NOTE: Such is the stench when *Amonphophallus* is in bloom that unless one has an area to isolate the plant, one could lose both friends and family.

Anemone coronaria

Anredera

Anemone species   WINDFLOWER   Rhizome
Ranunculaceae, North Temperate Zone

USES: Garden. *A. coronaria* also widely used for pots and cutting.

HABIT: *A. blanda* grows 2-8 inches high, with flowers in white, pink or blue produced in early spring. *A. x fulgens* has flowers among the brightest scarlet in all horticulture. *A. coronaria* grows to 18 inches, with large, poppy-like flowers, either single or double, in white, blue, pink and red, produced in late spring or summer and excellent for cutting.

CULTURE: Soak rhizomes in water for 24 hours prior to planting, then set out in the garden at a depth of 1-2 inches and 8-12 inches apart, in a perfectly drained soil and sunny location. *A. blanda* and *A. x fulgens* should be planted in fall, *A. coronaria* in fall or spring (the latter preferable in northern areas). Keep moist during the growing season. The first two species are fully hardy; *A. coronaria* should be lifted north of Zone 6 and stored dry at 70° over winter. Zone 6 and south, apply winter mulch.

NOTE: Some historians feel that the biblical "Lilies of the field" which "Toil not, neither do they spin" are, in fact, Anemones.

Anredera cordifolia   (Boussingaultia baselloides)   Tuberous Root
                            MADEIRA VINE
Basellaceae, South America   Zone 9

USES: Covering Trellises, Porches, Screening

HABIT: A rapidly growing, twining climber, often producing tubers in the axils of the leaves. It bears fragrant white flowers in long racemes during late summer.

CULTURE: Set out after danger of frost, 3-4 inches deep, in a rich, well-drained soil in full sun. Keep moist during the growing season, then dig and store at about 55° F. during winter. May also be used as a greenhouse subject, if space permits, as it may reach 20 feet in height.

Antigonon

Apios

Antigonon leptopus   CORAL or   Tuber
                           CONFEDERATE VINE
Polygonaceae, Mexico   Zone 10

USES: Screens, Trellises

HABIT: A vine, climbing by means of tendrils, and clad in light green, arrow-shaped leaves. Racemes of bright pink (or, in some forms, white), flowers are freely borne in summer. Plants may reach 40 feet in height.

CULTURE: Easily grown in virtually any soil. Requires full sun to bloom freely; keep evenly moist, supplying additional water during periods of drought.

NOTE: Tubers are said to be edible.

Apios americana   GROUNDNUT,   Tuberous Root
                        POTATO BEAN
Leguminosae, Eastern North America   Zone 4

USES: Wild Garden

HABIT: A twining vine with alternate, compound leaves, growing to about 8 feet in length and dying back to the ground each winter. Fragrant, brownish pea-shaped flowers are borne in clusters during late summer. The tuberous roots are edible, with a flavor somewhat resembling turnips.

CULTURE: Easily grown in ordinary garden soil in sun or light shade.

Arisaema   *Arisarum*

Arisaema species   Tuber
Araceae, Northern Hemisphere

USES: Wild or Shady Garden

HABIT: Plants with attractive lobed foliage, interesting and often oddly-formed flower spathes, and attractive berries. The species, of which many are excellent garden subjects, include two particularly familiar types. Jack-in-the-Pulpit, *A. triphyllum,* grows to 3 feet with single, 3-part lush leaves and hooded blossom spathes of greenish brown, followed by brilliant red berries in spikes. *A. Dracontium* (Green Dragon), has a bloom consisting of a long, greenish-yellow spadix surrounded by a green spathe, and multi-segmented foliage. It produces red berries in summer and fall.

CULTURE: Because the tubers develop roots from the top, they should be set quite deeply (to 4 inches) in a partially shaded location. The soil should be rich, humusy and moist. Plants become dormant in midsummer. In areas with late spring frosts, a winter mulch, left in place until danger of frost is gone, will help protect the tender young shoots. Plants do best when planted in fall.

Arisarum proboscideum   MOUSE PLANT   Rhizome
Araceae, Italy   Zone 5

USES: Ground Cover

HABIT: One of the most curious of all the plants of creation, growing about two inches in height, with single, ovate leaves. Its oddly contorted spathe is olive green tinged with brown, purple in the mouth, and it also has an ascending tail-like tip 4-6 inches long arising from the hood of the spath. The total effect is that the bloom resembles a rather futuristic mouse.

CULTURE: Grow in a rich, humusy soil that remains rather moist, setting the rhizomes about 3 inches below the surface. Partial shade suits it best, and it is an excellent ground cover to use in beds under broad-leaved evergreens.

Asarum   Asclepias

Asarum species   WILD GINGER   Rhizome
Aristolochiaceae, Northern Temperate Zone

USES: Wild Garden, Ground Cover

HABIT: A group of low-growing plants with usually heart-shaped leaves and brown or purplish, bell-shaped nodding flowers. They make excellent ground covers for shaded places, particularly as many of the species are evergreen. *A. Shuttleworthii* has attractively mottled, heart-shaped leaves and strangely bottle-shaped maroon flowers in spring. Its foliage often assumes a purplish cast in winter. *A. europaeum* has glossy green leaves, round or kidney-shaped, and grows to only 5 inches in height. Its flowers are greenish purple or brown, and it is among the most prized of evergreen ground covers for shade or semi-shade. *A. arifolium* has arrow-shaped, usually mottled leaves. *A. virginicum,* with purple flowers, has mottled evergreen leaves, while the hardiest of the species, *A. canadense,* has brownish-purple spring flowers and is deciduous.

CULTURE: Grow in full or partial shade in any good moist, garden soil, preferably of high organic content. Some species will perform well in sun if ample moisture is provided.

Asclepias tuberosa   BUTTERFLY WEED,   Tuberous Root
                              PLEURISY ROOT
Asclepiadaceae, U. S. A. and Northern Mexico   Zone 3

USES: Borders, Naturalized in Meadows

HABIT: Two to three-foot plants with rigid stems topped by large flat umbels usually of orange, but occasionally yellow or orange-red, during July and August. An excellent source of brilliant summer color when planted in mass.

CULTURE: Prefers a well-drained sunny location and flourishes in thin, poorly nourished soils. Indestructible once established, large clumps may be difficult to move. Plants are very late to break their dormancy in spring, so care should be taken not to remove them accidentally from the garden. Easily propagated from seed.

NOTE: The dried, powdered root has been used in folk medicine.

Begonia x hybrida 'Pendula'

Belamcanda

Begonia x tuberhybrida　　TUBEROUS ROOTED　　Tuber
　　　　　　　　　　　　　　　BEGONIA
Begoniaceae, derived from numerous Andean species

USES: Garden, Pots, Hanging Baskets

HABIT: Attractive, free flowering plants with hairy leaves often tinted red, and flowers, either single or double, in all colors except blue and purple. Flowers are of many forms including singles and doubles shaped variously like roses, narcissi, camellias or carnations. Solid colors and those with contrasting edges or blotches are available. Plant types include 12-18 inch upright plants, bushier ones to 10 inches (multiflora) and pendulous or hanging types. Tuberous begonias are among the most useful of plants for providing color all summer long in shaded or partially shaded locations.

CULTURE: While Tuberous Begonias may be planted directly in the garden well after the danger of frost, it is far more practical to start them indoors. Plant in flats or pots filled with peat or a peat-based planting mixture. Set tubers with concave side up, covering with no more than ½ inch of medium. Keep moist and provide bottom heat. After plants have started and all danger of frost is past, set outside in the garden in a partially shaded location where the soil is well-drained but provides ample moisture. Avoid exposure to wind, as stems are brittle. Keep moist throughout the growing season, preferably avoiding wetting the foliage or flowers. Fertilize several times during active growth (organic foods such as fish emulsion produce good results). When leaves yellow after first frost, lift, dry for several days, remove dirt and dead growth and store in dry peat at a temperature of 45-50° F.

Belamcanda species　　BLACKBERRY LILY　　Rhizome
Iridaceae, China and Japan　　　　　　　　　　Zone 5

USES: Garden, Dried Arrangements

HABIT: 1-4 foot plants with sword-shaped leaves and bearing clusters of brightly colored, often spotted flowers in late summer. These are followed by pods which open to reveal bunches of glossy black seeds that resemble blackberries and are most attractive in dried arrangements. *B. chinensis* grows to 3-4 feet and has deep orange flowers with red dots; *B. flabellata* to 18 inches with light yellow flowers spotted orange. *X Pardancanda Norrisii*, a bigeneric hybrid between *Belamcanda* and *Pardanthopsis,* grows to 2-5 feet with up to 2½ inch flowers in almost every imaginable color, many of them strikingly striped and dotted.

CULTURE: Plant in fall or spring in sun or light shade, setting rhizomes 1 inch deep and 6 inches apart. A light, sandy, well-drained soil is best. In northern areas, protect with a winter mulch.

Bletilla   *Bowiea*

Bletilla striata   CHINESE GROUND ORCHID   Rhizome
Orchidaceae, China and Japan   Zone 8

USES: Garden, Pots

HABIT: 6-10 Cattleya-shaped 1½ inch flowers, usually purple, but occasionally white, borne in June on 15-24 inch plants with prominently pleated foliage. (Commonly offered as *B. hyacinthina.*)

CULTURE: In the garden, plant in fall or spring, 4 inches deep and 4-6 inches apart. Best results are obtained when plants are grown in partial shade in a moist, well-drained, highly organic soil. Supply ample moisture during growing season. Mulch heavily for winter in colder areas.

In pots, start in fall or winter, planting in a highly organic potting medium. At first, keep completely shaded and grow at a night temperature of 50°, increasing to 60° and providing filtered light after growth starts.

Bowiea volubilis   CLIMBING ONION (Sea Onion)   Bulb
Liliaceae, South Africa   Zone 10

USES: Pots

HABIT: Grown as a curiosity, rather than for its great ornamental value. It produces green twining stems with sparse linear leaves resembling that of asparagus and small, greenish white flowers.

CULTURE: Pot the large, globular bulb so that at least half of it is above the surface of the standard potting mixture. Keep moist during active growth and provide a trellis for it to climb on. Allow to dry out from May to October, after which cycle is started again.

Brodiaea   *Caladium*

Brodiaea species and hybrids   Corm
Amaryllidaceae, Western North America   Zone 7

USES: Borders, Rock Gardens, Naturalizing, Pots

HABIT: Spring and summer blooming plants with grassy foliage and bright, funnel-shaped flowers, in a wide range of colors, but with purples and violets predominating the species. They grow 1-3 feet in height. Many hybrids are available. Allied genera include *Triteleia* and *Dichelostemma.*

CULTURE: In areas where hardy (Zone 7 and below), plant in fall, 2-3 inches deep and the same distance apart. A very well-drained, gravelly soil, completely free of manure, should be selected, but leaf mold or a slow-release fertilizer can be employed. Supply ample moisture during the growing season, then allow to dry off completely in summer. Apply winter mulch.

For pot culture, use well-drained, coarse potting mixture, barely covering the corms. Grow in a sunny situation, at a night temperature of 50° F. Outdoors, provide ample moisture while in active growth, then dry off by withholding water after flowering is finished.

Caladium x hortulanum   FANCY-LEAVED   Tuber
                                CALADIUM
Araceae, Tropical America   Zone 10

USES: Garden, Pots. Outstanding for bedding in shade.

HABIT: Lush plants with broadly arrow-shaped leaves in striking color combinations of reds, pinks, greens and white.

CULTURE: Start tubers indoors, in February or March, either in flats or pots in a peaty medium. Plant with knobby side up, covering with 2 inches of medium. Provide ample moisture and supply bottom heat to facilitate sprouting as 75-80° F. will best promote growth. For garden use, when nights no longer drop below 60° F., transplant to a shaded location in the garden, plunging pots in soil to the level of the rim. Drainage must be good, but supply ample water and syringe foliage with water on hot days. For best growth, remove the rather insignificant flowers as they form. In early fall, gradually withhold water until leaves die back, dry tubers several days in a well-ventilated, shady area, and store in dry peat at 65-70° F.

Calochortus

Calochortus species	MARIPOSA LILY, BUTTERFLY TULIP	Bulb
Liliaceae, Western North America		Zone 5

USES: Garden

HABIT: Narrow-leaved plants 8-24 inches tall, bearing cup or globe-shaped flowers, variously from March-June and in a wide range of colors and color combinations. The species vary widely as to flower form and coloration including: *C. albus,* from Northern California, with flowers white or white tinged with rose, growing to 2½ feet; *C. Tolmiei,* Central California to Washington, 16 inches with white or cream flowers, sometimes marked with pink or purple; *C. clavatus,* growing to 2 feet with yellow flowers marked red-brown; *C.Gunnisonii,* from the Rocky Mountains, with lavender tinted white flowers on 18 inch stems; *C. Kennedyi,* from the deserts of the Southwest, whose brilliant vermilion flowers are among the brightest in the plant kingdom; *C. luteus,* 18 inches tall with deep yellow flowers marked brown; *C. macrocarpus,* from the Pacific Northwest, with purple flowers banded in green on 20 inch stems; *C. Nuttallii* (Sega Lily), the state flower of Utah, with blooms of white, yellow or pink; *C. Plummerae,* from Southern California with pink or lavender flowers with hairy petals, borne on 16 inch plants; and *C. venustus,* the Mariposa of the early Spanish explorers, with flowers of white, pink, yellow, lavender or wine-red on 2 foot plants. As a rule, Calochortus is offered for sale as a mixture, including many species and hybrids.

CULTURE: Plant in late fall, so as to prevent premature fall growth. Select a gravelly, extra-well-drained soil that has been well enriched with organic matter. Set bulbs at a depth of 2-3 inches and the same distance apart. Apply a winter mulch immediately after planting and remove in spring. Calochortus requires extremely dry conditions in the summer and early fall. In areas with heavy rainfall during that time of year, it may be well to dig bulbs after the flowers have faded and store dry until planting time late in fall.

NOTE: *C. Nuttallii* provided the early Mormon settlers of Utah with food, as the bulbs were cooked in a variety of ways.

Camassia

Canna

Camassia species   CAMAS, QUAMASH   Bulb
Liliaceae, North America   Zone 3

USES: Garden, Naturalizing

HABIT: Plants with grassy leaves and growing 1½-4 feet in height, bearing 6-segmented, star-shaped flowers in shades of blue or white. Bloom in late spring. *C. Cusickii* grows about 18 inches tall, with flowers pale blue to violet-blue. *C. Leichtlinii* reaches 4 feet in height with white, blue or violet blue blossoms. *C. Quamash (C. esculenta)* is 2½ feet tall with flowers in the same color range. *C. scilloides* (Wild Hyacinth or Indigo Squill) is of the same height and coloration and is a more easterly native.

CULTURE: Plant in fall in sun or light shade, 4 inches deep and 8-10 inches apart. A fairly heavy, well-drained soil that will provide ample moisture during the growing season is preferred. In warm areas, delay planting until November to prevent premature fall growth. Never allow to lack moisture, and do not disturb established plantings.

NOTE: Bulbs of *Camassia* (especially *C. Quamash*) constituted a staple in the diet of the Indians of the Pacific Northwest, particularly the Nez Perce.

Canna x generalis   INDIAN SHOT   Rhizome
Cannaceae, Tropical and Subtropical America   Zone 7

USES: Garden, Formal Beds, Containers

HABIT: Plants 1½-5 feet tall, with broad, 6-12 inch leaves in bright green, blue-green or glossy bronze. Flower spikes up to 1 foot long are produced from early summer until frost, and bear numerous 4-5 inch flowers in shades of yellow, orange, pink and red.

CULTURE: In northern areas, where growing season is short, Cannas may be started indoors in the same manner as Tuberous-rooted Begonias. Otherwise, plant after danger of frost at a depth of 3-4 inches and 1½-3 feet apart, in a rich, humusy soil that will provide ample moisture. Cannas enjoy heat and should be grown in full sun. North of Zone 7, after frost has blackened foliage, cut back, dig, dry and store over winter upside down at 50-60° F. In Zone 7 and south, they may be left in the ground over winter, but should be divided every 3-4 years.

NOTE: The black seeds are so hard that they were used as shot by early colonists of the U. S., hence the common name.

Cardiocrinum

Chionodoxa

Cardiocrinum species
Liliaceae, Asia

Bulb
Zone 6

USES: Garden, Edible

HABIT: Tall plants, formerly classified with the true lilies, with heart-shaped leaves and predominantly white, trumpet-shaped flowers in summer. The main bulbs die at the end of the year, but are replaced by offsets. Species include: *C. cathayanum,* often listed as *Lilium cathayanum,* from Central and Eastern China, which grows 1-4 feet with flowers greenish-white on the reverse, white or cream spotted with purple inside; *C. cordatum (Lilium cordatum),* from Japan, 4-6 feet in height with cream-white petals striped with yellow and a reddish-brown spotted throat. It is widely grown for its edible bulbs. *C. giganteum (Lilium giganteum),* from Burma, Nepal and Tibet, is the largest of the genus, growing 6-12 feet with a basal rosette of heart-shaped leaves. The flowers are greenish-white on the reverse; the inside is red-purple spotted with white.

CULTURE: Grow in a cool, partially shaded location, in a rich soil that remains constantly moist. Cover bulbs with only 1 inch of soil and apply winter mulch.

Chionodoxa species   GLORY-OF-THE-SNOW
Liliaceae, Asia Minor and The Aegean Region

Bulb
Zone 3

USES: Border, Mass Plantings, Naturalizing

HABIT: 5-8 inch, early spring blooming plants bearing clusters of short-tubular, bell-shaped flowers. *C. Luciliae* is most commonly blue with a white center, but pink and white forms are grown. *C. sardensis* has flowers of pale blue without the white center. The foliage is grass-like.

CULTURE: Plant in fall, selecting a very well-drained soil in sun or partial shade. Plant in masses, 3 inches deep and about the same distance apart. Good drainage and ample moisture during the growing season is essential. *Chionodoxas* spread rapidly, both from offset bulbs and from seeds.

Claytonia *Clivia*

Claytonia species SPRING BEAUTY Corm
Portulacaceae, North America Zone 4

USES: Wild Garden, Spring Ground Cover, Rock Garden

HABIT: Low growing succulent plants with white or pink spring flowers, and usually somewhat linear leaves. *C. caroliniana* grows to about 1 foot, has broader leaves than others of the genus, and has pink or white blooms. *C. lanceolata* grows about 10 inches high with white or pink flowers marked with yellow. *C. virginica* has white to pink flowers and grows to about 1 foot. The succulent leaves remain green during the winter, then die back shortly after the plants have flowered.

CULTURE: Grown in a moist, shaded location, or under deciduous trees where they will receive some winter sun, *Claytonias* will quickly form large colonies and serve as a fine ground cover. Plant 3-4 inches deep and about 8 inches apart, then leave undisturbed.

Clivia miniata, varieties and hybrids Tuberous Root
KAFFIR LILY
Amaryllidaceae, South Africa Zone 10

USES: Pots, Containers

HABIT: Plants with deep green, strap-shaped evergreen leaves and clusters of orange to scarlet, lily-like flowers borne on 2 foot stems, usually from May to July.

CULTURE: Plant in pots filled with a rich potting mixture, setting roots just below the surface. Water generously in spring and summer, less often in fall and winter. Containers may be set out in a partially shaded location during frost-free periods. Feed during spring and summer with a soluble plant food. Grows best when potbound. High humidity during active growth and a night temperature of 50° F. give best results. From October to January, *Clivia* enters a semi-resting period, and watering should be reduced, but not to the point where the leaves begin to wither.

Colchicum   Colchicum (Double Form)

Colchicum species   MEADOW SAFFRON   Corm
Liliaceae, Europe, North Africa, Asia Minor   Zone 4

USES: Garden, Pots

HABIT: Large flower chalices, somewhat resembling giant crocuses, borne on leafless 6-8 inch stems. Many are late-summer-and fall-blooming, and these bloom without the large, rather coarse leaves which appear in spring and die back in June. The spring-blooming species produce leaves and flowers at the same time. The more widely-grown, fall-blooming species include: *C. autumnale,* with flowers of purple or white (some double forms are found), *C. byzantium,* with lavender-pink flowers, *C. giganteum,* blooms of rosy-purple, and *C. speciosum* which includes white, rose, purple and dark red types. Spring blooming species include *C. fasciculare* with white to pink blooms and *C. luteum,* a yellow.

CULTURE: Plant corms in August, 3-4 inches deep and 9-12 inches apart in a rich, gritty, well-drained soil with high humus content. *Colchicum* requires ample moisture, particularly in the spring when foliage is growing. They are among the easiest of all "bulbous" plants to force and will even flower (although not as well as if grown normally) if left unplanted set on a dish or blotter on the windowsill.

NOTE: The name "Meadow Saffron" is deceptive. *Colchicum* is not the source of saffron—far from it, the corms are toxic. Malingering Greek slaves used to eat them to induce illness which would excuse them from labor. Wine of Colchicum, an old remedy for gout, is derived from the corms, as is the alkaloid Colchicine, used in plant breeding to bring about ploidy or changes in chromosome count.

Colocasia

Convallaria

Colocasia esculenta　　　ELEPHANT'S-EAR,　　　Corm
　　　　　　　　　　　　　　TARO, DASHEEN
Araceae, Tropical Asia and Pacific Oceania　　　Zone 10

USES: Garden Background, Containers, Food Crop

HABIT: Lush, 3 to 7 foot plants bearing huge, heart-shaped green leaves up to 2 feet across. Flowers are of little ornamental consequence.

　　　　CULTURE: Plant in spring, after all danger of frost is past, choosing a very rich, moist, highly organic soil in full sun or light shade. Set corms 2-3 inches deep and 3-6 feet apart. Apply slow-release fertilizer. May be started indoors, 4-6 weeks before outdoor planting time, in peat with ample bottom heat provided. Prefers very ample water and high humidity. Before frost, dig corms, dry and store in dry sawdust or perlite at 50° F.

NOTE: *Colocasia* is widely grown as a major food crop throughout Asia and the Pacific Islands. The young shoots are sometimes blanched and eaten as a potherb, and, more important, the corms are grated, mixed with water, allowed to ferment and served as "poi". Poi is the equivalent of the grits of our South, at best barely edible. Its widespread use as a food merely proves how hardy and/or desperate for food are those who use it!

Convallaria majalis　　　LILY-OF-THE-VALLEY　　　Rhizome
Liliaceae, Temperate Northern Hemisphere　　　Zones 3-7

USES: Garden, Naturalizing, Ground Cover, Pots, Cutting

HABIT: 6-8 inch plants with 2 leaves and stems with typically white, highly fragrant, pendulous, bell-shaped flowers borne in May. Double flowered and pink cultivars, as well as one with variegated foliage, are occasionally offered in the trade.

CULTURE: Plant in late fall in a shady location. A moist, highly organic soil produces the best results, and the liberal addition of manure will increase flower production and plant vigor. Set 1 inch deep and 4-6 inches apart. Top dress annually with leaf mold or well-rotted manure. Dig and divide every 4 years.

"Pips" that have been specially prepared by freezing are readily available for forcing in pots or in the greenhouse. Select a pot 3 inches deep and fill with a peat-based potting mixture. Cut approximately 1/3 of the roots away, and plant with the "pip" or pinkish crown just above the surface of the medium. Water thoroughly and grow fairly cool. Flowers can be expected in three weeks from such planting.

Corydalis

Costus

Corydalis FUMEWORT Rhizome, Tuber
Fumariaceae, North Temperate Zone Zone 4

USES: Border, Wild Garden

HABIT: A group of plants, closely related to Dicentra, often with attractive, fern-like foliage, sometimes bluish or grayish, and pendulous flowers in spring or summer. Not all the species are tuberous or rhizomatous; we mention only those that are. They include: *C. bulbosa,* from Europe and Asia, with racemes of purple, rose or white flowers; *C. aurea,* an American native with pendulous yellow blooms; *C. nobilis,* from Central Asia, among the tallest, with yellow flowers tipped in brown; *C. Souleri,* from the Pacific Northwest, with pink or white blooms, the plants tending to become invasive; and *C. saxicola,* with yellowish-green leaves and large yellow flowers. The latter is less hardy than the others mentioned.

CULTURE: While *Corydalis* will grow well in full sun, its blooming period tends to be shorter than if planted in partial shade. Plant about 1 foot apart in any garden soil. Requires little care.

Costus speciosus SPIRAL GINGER, Rhizome
  CREPE GINGER
Zingiberaceae, East Indies Zone 10

USES: Pots

HABIT: A lush, tall plant to 10 feet, with spirally arranged, glabrous, oval leaves. The flowers are borne in dense, curving spikes with green and red bracts and white flowers with yellow centers. While rather large for most house plant collections, it is graceful and striking and elicits comment wherever it is seen.

CULTURE: Plant in large tub filled with rich soil and grow under conditions of filtered light at warm temperatures, keeping constantly moist. During the warmer portions of the year, or in southern Florida, it may be grown outside in partial shade.

Crocus

Crocus species and hybrids   Corm
Iridaceae, Mediterranean Europe and Africa, Near East   Zone 3

USES: Border, Rock Garden, Naturalizing, Pots

HABIT: Small plants with grasslike foliage, keeled on the surface and often with a thin white midrib on the upper surface. The tepals are six in number and form a graceful chalice. Crocuses may be divided into two groups, spring and fall blooming; the former flower from February to April, the latter from September to November. Many, particularly the fall-blooming types, flower before the foliage appears. Plants are from 2 to 6 inches in height and include various shades of lavender and purple, white, and (primarily for spring-bloomers) yellow. Fall blooming species include: *C. asturicus* from Spain, various shades of lavender; *C. cancellatus,* white striped lavender or yellow striped purple; *C. hadriaticus,* from Greece, white with yellow throat and purple markings; *C. longiflorus,* lavender with orange throat; *C. laevigatus,* lavender flushed with red-purple and fragrant, *C. medius,* from the Alps, with deep purple blooms; *C. ochroleucus,* cream-white with yellow center; *C. sativus* (Saffron Crocus), pinkish lavender and fragrant; *C. speciosus,* lavender veined purple (a white form is in the trade), and *C. Kotschyanus (C. zonatus),* rosy lavender. Most widely grown of the spring flowering sorts are the "Dutch Crocus", whose cultivars include shades of purple and lavender, white, white striped with purple and yellow. Many of these may be hybrid forms between *C. vernus* and other species. Many of the other spring bloomers flower even earlier than the ubiquitous *C. vernus, C. luteus* is bright orange-yellow; *C. angustifolius, C. susianus,* Cloth-of-Gold Crocus is an early-blooming bright yellow; *C. biflorus* blooms early in white or shades of lavender and white or combinations thereof; *C. chrysanthus* ranges from pale cream to soft yellow; *C. Tomasinianus* is lavender and *C. versicolor* is purple, white, or white striped with purple.

CULTURE: *Crocus* do best in cool areas. Plant 2-4 inches deep and 4 inches apart in a well-drained soil of low fertility, in full sun or very light shade. Spring bloomers are planted in fall, fall-bloomers in late summer. Under good conditions, and if untroubled by rodents, which are a major problem, *crocus* will multiply rapidly to form large, attractive colonies. Foliage should be allowed to ripen naturally before being cut back.

Spring blooming *crocus* may also be forced in pots. Set 5-6 to a 5 inch pot, using a well-drained medium and covering the corms 1 inch deep. Pre-cool in the cold frame for about 6 weeks, then bring indoors and grow in a sunny situation with a night temperature of about 50° F.

NOTE: One species of fall-blooming *Crocus, C. sativus,* is now, and was in the past even more so, of commercial importance as the source of saffron. Derived from the dried stigmas, saffron is used to dye and flavor foods and, in olden times for medicinal purposes. Major centers where *C. sativus* was grown included Crete, Persia, and parts of England.

Crocosmia   Cyclamen

Crocosmia species and hybrids   MONTEBRETIA   Corm
Iridaceae, South Africa   Zone 6

USES: Garden, Cutting, Pots

HABIT: Sword-shaped foliage and loose spikes of gladiolus-like flowers in various bright colors and reaching 4 feet in height. Blooms in late summer. *C. aurea,* rarely offered, has yellow flowers flushed apricot and orange; *C. Masoniorum* has vermilion-orange flowers set atop its arching stems; *C. Pottsii* has smaller orange flowers marked with yellow. *C. x crocosmiiflora,* a hybrid between *C. aurea* and *C. Pottsii,* is widely offered in the trade in a number of colors from yellow through orange to red, often with attractive markings.

CULTURE: In the garden, plant in late spring in sun (preferable) or partial shade, setting the corms 3 inches deep and about the same distance apart. Any soil that provides adequate drainage will do. Fertilize lightly during the growing season. In areas where it is hardy, *Crocosmia* will colonize rapidly, so division every few years is necessary. In colder areas, dig and store dry at a temperature of 70° F. over winter.

In pots, plant 6 corms ½ inch deep in a 5 inch pot. Water and set in a cool cellar or cold frame until growth begins, then transfer to a bright window and water freely during growth.

NOTE: *Crocosmia* has recently been crossed with *Curtonus* to produce some bigeneric hybrids of exceptional promise, both as garden subjects and as a possible cutflower crop.

Cyclamen species   Tuber
Primulaceae, Central Europe, Mediterranean Region   Zone 6
                Asia Minor

USES: Garden, Rock Garden (hardy species), Pots

HABIT: Known to all is the showy Florist's Cyclamen, *C. persicum,* with its heart-shaped leaves, often attractively marked with silver, and large reflexed flowers borne well above the foliage. There are many cultivars, varying in size and foliage, with colors ranging from white through various shades of pink, to reds and purples. There are also numerous "eyed" or bicolor ones. Smaller and less flamboyant are the hardy species, charming dwarf plants with leaves usually marbled on the upper surface and often red on the lower side. Blooms are white or various shades of pink or red. *C. cilicium* blooms in late summer and fall, with fragrant pink flowers marked with crimson at the base. *C. hederifolium (C. neopolitanum)* has white or pink flowers, again with

Cyclamen | Dahlia

crimson blotch, in late summer and autumn. *C. purpurascens (C. europaeum)* is distinguished for its exceptionally fragrant pink or rose blooms in late summer. *C. repandum* is a spring bloomer, with white, pink or red flowers.

CULTURE: Widely used as a gift plant for Christmas or Valentine's Day, *C. persicum* is a pot plant only; but a pot plant difficult to maintain under normal household conditions. It requires cool night temperatures, rarely exceeding 50°. Commercially, it is grown from seeds, requiring 15-18 months from sowing to maturity, or sometimes from tubers.

The hardy Cyclamens are best grown in a partially shaded garden location, in a well-drained soil containing leaf mold and sand. During their period of summer dormancy, little water should be present.

Dahlia species and cultivars   Tuberous Root
Compositae, Mexico, Columbia and Central America   Zone 10

USES: Garden, Cutting

HABIT: 2-8 foot plants flowering in late summer and fall, and producing flowers up to 10 inches across. A wide range of colors (excepting blue) and types are available. Botanical origins are confused; the *Dahlia* of today is the product of ages of breeding, using many species.

CULTURE: Select a sunny location with a well-drained soil. Dig a hole 8-10 inches deep, replace 2 inches of soil, lay in the *Dahlia* root, and place a stake 1 inch away from the "eye". Cover root with 2 inches of soil and fertilize lightly. As growth progresses, gradually add soil until flush with the level of the bed. Prune plant to a single stem and pinch out many of the side shoots to promote larger flowers. Excessive applications of fertilizer may delay flowering. A summer mulch will keep roots cool and preserve moisture. After frost blackens foliage, dig, clean off dirt and remove growth, then store at 60° dry or in sawdust.

NOTE: Roots are used as food in remote areas of Mexico.

Dicentra eximia

Dichelostemma

Dicentra species   BLEEDING-HEART   Rhizome, Tuber
Fumariaceae, North America, Asia   Zone 3

USES: Border, Wild Garden

HABIT: Plants with attractive compound or dissected foliage, racemes of pendulous flowers in various shades of pink and white. *D. canadensis* (Squirrel Corn) grows to 1 ft. with finely cut foliage and fragrant white flowers tinged with purple in spring. *D. Cucullaria* (Dutchman's Breeches) are plants under 1 foot tall with basal leaves and white flowers in spring. Plants go dormant after flowering. *D. eximia,* grows to 2 feet with basal, fern-like foliage and pink to rose flowers produced all spring and summer. Several improved hybrids based on *D. eximia* are available. *D. spectabilis* (Showy Bleeding Heart) attains 2 feet or more in height with pendant flowers of rose-pink or occassionally white, borne in pendulous racemes in spring. Native to Japan.

CULTURE: Grow in soil enriched with organic matter, with an ample supply of moisture in sun or partial shade. Perpetual blooming types, such as *D. eximia,* many bloom only sparsely during extremely hot weather. A summer mulch will serve to conserve moisture and keep soil cool.

Dichelostemma species   Corm
Amaryllidaceae, Western North America   Zone 7

USES: Garden

HABIT: Low perennial herbs with linear leaves, distinguished by a prominent midrib that produces a keeled effect. The flowers are borne in tightly packed umbels. Closely related to *Brodiaea. D. congestum* has soft lavender blooms and grows 1-3 feet tall; *D. Ida-Maia* (Firecracker Flower) grows to 3 feet with brilliant red blooms; *D. volubile* is a twining plant to 5 feet with pink blooms. All flower in spring.

CULTURE: In areas where hardy (Zone 7 and below), plant in fall, 2-3 inches deep and the same distance apart. A very well-drained, gravely soil, completely free of manure, should be selected, but leaf mold or a slow-release fertilizer should be employed. Supply ample moisture during the growing season, then allow to dry off completely in summer. Apply winter mulch.

For pot culture, use well-drained coarse potting mixture, barely covering the corms. Grow in a sunny situation, at a night temperature of 50° F. Outdoors, provide ample moisture while in active growth, then dry-off after flowering.

Dietes

Dioscorea elephantipes

Dietes species   Rhizome
Iridaceae, Tropical and South Africa   Zone 10

USES: Garden (where hardy), Pots

HABIT: Plants with fans of sword-shaped or linear leaves and short-lived Iris-like flowers. *D. bicolor* has lemon-yellow flowers with a brown basal spot, *D. grandiflora,* large orange flowers marked with brown and violet, *D. Robinsoniana,* white flowers, and *D. vegeta,* white flowers marked with yellow or brown and blue.

CULTURE: In the garden, where hardy, plant at any time, setting 18 to 24 inches apart at the same depth as they previously grew (note the soil line). Grow in full sun. Moisture requirements vary with the species, but all require good drainage.

To grow in pots, add additional drainage material (pot shards, gravel, etc.), to the bottom of a pot, then plant in a well-drained mixture. Grow in a sunny situation, at a night temperature of 60-65° F., keeping moist and feeding every month with a soluble fertilizer. Reduce watering during winter months.

Dioscorea species   YAM   Tuberous Root
Dioscoreaceae, Tropics and Subtropics World-Wide   Zone 10

USES: Pots, Food Crops

HABIT: Twining, sometimes woody vines with lush foliage and tuberous roots, many of which are edible. Many are grown as major food sources, others as ornamentals, still others combine the two. *D. Batatas,* native to E. Asia and hardy to Zone 5, referred to as Chinese Yam or Cinnamon Vine, is grown in the Orient for food, but in America as an ornamental. *D. bulbifera,* from tropical Asia, is remarkable for having tubers in the axils of the leaves. Some varieties are edible. *D. discolor,* from Central America, has attractive, large heart-shaped leaves, green above, marbled with light green and silver, and purple below. *D. elephantipes* (Elephant's Foot), is grown as a curiosity for its large woody, knobby tuber, and is sometimes eaten in times of dire need by the indigenous population. *D. villosa,* with hairy, cordate leaves is native to the Eastern United States.

CULTURE: Where hardy, plant at any time of year by planting a piece of the tuberous root 3-5 inches deep in a rich soil capable of retaining an ample amount of moisture. Constant moisture is essential even though good drainage is required.

NOTE: In addition to their use as edibles and ornamentals, several species are used in pharmocology.

Dionaea

Disporum flavescens

Dionaea muscipula   VENUS-FLYTRAP   Rhizome
Droseraceae, The Carolinas   Zone 7

USES: Pot Plant, Terrarium

HABIT: One of the carnivorous plants, native to the swamps of North and South Carolina, growing 8 to 10 inches high with, leaves arranged in rosettes. The leaves, edged with curving bristles, are hinged and close around insects which are attracted by the crimson secretion of the leaves. Leaves are reddish in full sun, green in the shade. White flowers, borne 4-10 on 8-10 inch stalks, are produced in June.

CULTURE: Venus Flytrap requires constantly high humidity, ample moisture, acid soil and ample light. Take a 4-5 inch pot, fill bottom third with pebbles, then add a layer of moistened peat based planting mixture, then a layer of moistened unmilled sphagnum moss. Plant so that just the bottom portion of the rhizome is in the sphagnum, water and set pot in a saucer filled with water. Under conditions of low humidity, a cover of glass or plastic to conserve humidity will prove beneficial. For this reason, terrarium culture will prove effective. Set in a sunny location, or grow under fluorescent light, and remove flower stalks as they appear, as flowering tends to weaken the plant. A night temperature of 55-60° F. is best. In fall and winter, plants enter a resting period, so reduce watering, providing only enough to keep "bulbs" plump.

Disporum species   FAIRY BELLS, MANDARIN   Rhizome
Liliaceae, North America and Asia   Zone 3

USES: Wild Garden

HABIT: Plants to 2½ feet in height with large, prominently-veined ovate leaves and flowers in loose umbels in late spring, followed by often showy fruit. *D. Hookeri* (Fairy Bells) from California and Oregon, has white or greenish-white flowers and scarlet fruit; *D. lanuginosum,* (Yellow Mandarin), an Eastern species, yellow-green flowers and red fruit; *D. maculatum,* (Nodding Mandarin), also from the Eastern U.S.A., white flowers spotted with purple and yellow fruit; *D. Smithii,* (Fairy Lantern), white flowers and orange or red fruit. The loveliest in our opinion, *D. flavescens,* comes from Korea and has yellow flowers.

CULTURE: Plant spring or fall in a shady location and a neutral or acid soil, rich in humus. Requires good drainage, but soil should not be dry. A slope provides the ideal setting. A summer mulch will conserve moisture and keeps the soil cool. Spreads from seeds, too.

Dracunculus

Drosera

Dracunculus species   DRAGON LILY   Tuber
Araceae, Mediterranean Region   Zone 7

USES: Garden, Pots

HABIT: *D. vulgaris* grows to about 3 feet in height with mottled stems and bold fan-shaped divided leaves, often with white spots. It produces a huge red-purple spathe and maroon spadix. As with *Amorphophallus,* the flowers have a foul, carrion odor. Clusters of bright red berries follow. *D. canariensis,* from the Canary Islands, has a green spathe and yellow spadix.

CULTURE: In the garden, where hardy, plant about 4 inches deep and 18 inches apart in full sun and a well-drained soil. Provide ample water and winter mulch.

As a pot or container plant, use standard potting mixtures, covering the tubers about 2 inches deep in standard potting medium. Grow in a fairly sunny situation, ideally shaded from direct midday sun, with a night temperature of 60-65° F. Keep on the dry side until growth appears, then increase water and feed regularly with soluble plant food. After flowering, gradually withhold water so leaves will wilt. Restart cycle in fall.

Drosera species   SUNDEW   Rhizome
Droseraceae, World-wide

USES: Bog Garden, Terrarium

HABIT: Small herbaceous plants with spoon-shaped or thread-like leaves, covered with glistening hairs which exude a sticky fluid. This catches and digests insects which are absorbed by these carnivorous plants. Native species include *D. rotundifolia,* with spoon-shaped leaves, red hairs and white flowers; *D. filiformis* has thread-like leaves and purple flowers. There are also many exotic species from Africa and Australia.

CULTURE: Outdoors Droseras require a highly acid medium—a mixture of sphagnum and sand produces the best results—and a constant supply of water, along with high humidity. Bog or swamp gardens can provide these conditions, the conventional border cannot.

Indoors, they are best grown in a terrarium or pot tented over with a plastic bag. Use a sand base, then a thick layer of moist, unmilled sphagnum moss, covering rhizomes to the depth of about one inch. If a pot is used, stand it in a dish of water to help keep it constantly moist; an enclosed terrarium will achieve this on its own. Grow in filtered light and a fairly cool (55-60° F.), night temperature. Try to avoid watering with hard water.

Endymion

Epimedium

Endymion hispanicus	SILLA CAMPANULATA, WOOD HYACINTH	Bulb

Liliaceae, Western Europe and Northwestern Africa   Zone 4

USES: Garden, Naturalizing

HABIT: Spring blooming plants with spikes 12-18 inches high bearing nodding, bell-shaped flowers in shades of purple, blue and pink as well as white. Strap-shaped foliage.

CULTURE: Grows well in sun or, better still, partial shade. Once established, *Endymion* will spread rapidly, establishing attractive mass colonies. Plant in fall, 3-4 inches deep and 6 inches apart in a well-drained soil.

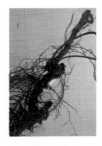

Epimedium species   Rhizome
Berberidaceae, Temperate Europe and Asia   Zone 5

USES: Ground cover, edging, rock garden. Effective massed under trees.

HABIT: Plants with light green, finely divided leaves that are bronzy red in spring. They grow to a height of less than a foot and are covered with graceful spurred flowers in loose sprays during May and June. *E. grandiflorum* flowers in white, pink, red or violet, *E. pinnatum* has bright yellow flowers with red spurs.

CULTURE: Prefer a moist, highly organic soil, acid in reaction and not necessarily of high fertility. They do best in partial shade, but will succeed in full shade or sun, the latter if kept amply moist.

Eranthis   *Eremurus at Sissinghurst Gardens*

| **Eranthis species and hybrids** | WINTER ACONITE | Tuber |
| *Ranunculaceae,* Europe and Asia Minor | | Zone 4 |

USES: Border, Rock Garden, Naturalizing

HABIT: Among the earliest blooming of all the spring bulbous plants, flowering in February and March. Plants are 2-8 inches in height with palmately divided leaves, and bears buttercup-like flowers. Those most readily available are the species *E. hyemalis,* with bright yellow flowers on 2-6 inch plants, and the larger hybrid *E. x Tubergenii,* whose yellow blossoms measure up to 3 inches in diameter. A white species, *E. pinnatifida,* is rarely offered in the trade.

CULTURE: Plant in early fall, as soon as tubers are obtainable. Soak them overnight in water before planting, then set 2-3 inches deep and 3-4 inches apart, in sun or light shade. A moist but well-drained soil, high in humus content, should be selected. Performs best in cool climates.

| **Eremurus species and hybrids** | FOXTAIL LILY | Tuberous Root |
| *Liliaceae,* Western and Central Asia | | Zone 5 |

USES: Garden Background, Cutting

HABIT: From thick, octopus-like roots spring tall, narrow stalks surrounded by sword-shaped basal leaves and bearing long racemes of 6-segmented flowers, usually in June and July. Plants are somewhat similar to the Yuccas. Species in common cultivation include: *E. Elwesii,* 6-9 feet with flowers of pink or white, *E. himalaicus,* 3 foot plants with white flowers, *E. robustus,* to 10 feet with bright pink blooms, *E. spectabilis,* to 3 feet with yellow flowers, and *E. stenophyllus (auranticacus)* 2 feet with yellow flowers. In addition, two groups of hybrids are widely grown: *E. x isabellinus,* (a cross between the species from Turkestan, *E. Olgae* and *E. stenophyllus*) with flowers of yellow, orange, pink or white on plants to 8 feet and *E. x Him-Rob* (a cross between *E. himalaicus* and *E. robustus*) usually retaining the relatively dwarf characteristics of the former and available in various pastels.

CULTURE: Plant in early fall in a sunny, well-drained location which will provide ample moisture during the growing season. Dig a hole 2 feet deep and 18 inches in diameter, with a conical mound in the center. Handling carefully, so as not to break the root, set the crown on the mound and spread the roots down into the hole. Fill with gritty soil, high in humus, until crown is covered 4-6 inches. Water thoroughly and apply a coarse mulch immediately. *Eremurus* thrives on heat. It should be left undisturbed once planted.

Erythronium

Erythronium

Erythronium species   DOG-TOOTH VIOLET,   Corm
                            TROUT LILY
Liliaceae, Temperate North America   Zone 3

USES: Garden, Wild Garden, Rock Garden, Naturalizing

HABIT: Nodding, star-shaped, lily-like flowers on 6-24 inch plants, blooming in April and May in shades of white, cream, pink, yellow and purple. Leaves are often attractively mottled in purple or brown. The corms, shaped like a canine tooth, give rise to one of the popular names. Species include: *E. americanum* (Adder's Tongue), an eastern variety with mottled leaves and graceful yellow flowers; *E. californicum,* from the West, with mottled leaves and white flowers marked with yellow, orange or brown; *E. grandiflorum,* from the Pacific Northwest, plain leaves, yellow or white blooms; *E. multiscapoideum,* mottled leaves and white flowers (N. California); *E. Hendersonii,* from California, with lavender flowers marked yellow and mottled leaves; *C. tuolumnense,* another California native, with light green leaves and golden yellow blooms.

CULTURE: Plant corms as early in the fall as you can obtain them, selecting a semi-shaded site with a rich, humusy soil. While ample moisture should be present, good drainage is necessary. Set 3 inches deep and 3-5 inches apart, then mulch to conserve moisture. Under these conditions, if left undisturbed, they will establish handsome colonies. Many of the western species are difficult to grow at low altitudes.

NOTE: Virtually within the shadow of the Empire State Building, there flows a magnificent trout stream, the Amawalk River. One of the author's most pleasant memories is, while walking along the bank of the stream, fly rod in hand, coming across a magnificent group of *E. americanum* in bloom.

Eucharis   *Eucomis*

Eucharis grandiflora   AMAZON LILY   Bulb
Amaryllidaceae, Colombia and Peru   Zone 9

USES: Containers, Pots, Cutting

HABIT: White, fragrant, narcissus-like flowers borne in umbels during late winter and early spring on 1-2 foot stems. The basal leaves are glossy and evergreen.

CULTURE: Plant 4-6 bulbs to an 8-10 inch pot, using a well-drained highly organic mixture and setting bulbs with their necks above the surface of the medium. Set in bright, filtered light (not full sun). Water sparingly until growth starts, then increase moisture. Grow at 65-70° night temperature under conditions of high humidity. When foliage starts to die back, reduce watering and keep dry during dormancy. *Eucharis* flowers best when potbound.

Eucomis comosa   PINEAPPLE LILY   Bulb
Liliaceae, South Africa   Zone 7

USES: Pots, Containers

HABIT: Green or white star-shaped flowers, clustered on 12-24 inch stems and topped by green sterile leaf bracts. The overall effect resembles a pineapple. The basal leaves are strap-shaped, with wavy margins and undersides spotted purple. Blooms late summer and early fall.

CULTURE: Plant in March, 1 bulb per 5 inch pot, using a sandy, well-drained potting mixture and barely covering the bulb. Water moderately until growth starts, then increase watering and apply a soluble fertilizer. After flowers have faded, reduce watering, barely keeping soil from drying out.

Ferraria

Freesia

Ferraria crispa
Iridaceae, South and Central Africa

Corm
Zone 7

USES: Pots, Garden

HABIT: Late spring- and summer-blooming plants about 18 inches tall, with sword-shaped leaves and somewhat cup-shaped flowers resembling orchids and interestingly colored in greenish brown spotted with purple. The individual blooms last only one day, but follow each other for several weeks. Flowers have a somewhat strange odor, suggestive of chocolate.

CULTURE: Plant in spring after nights no longer drop below 55° F. Set in a sunny location, in a well-drained soil, 3-4 inches deep and 4-8 inches apart. Keep soil moist and top-dress with 5-10-5 several times in the course of the growing season. In Zone 7 and south, bulbs may be over-wintered in the ground, lifting and dividing every 3-4 years. North of Zone 7, dig bulbs after foliage yellows, dry, remove dead foliage and store in dry peat or perlite at 60° F. over winter.

Freesia x hybrida
Iridaceae, South Africa

Corm
Zone 9

USES: Pots, Cutting

HABIT: Plants with sword-shaped leaves and wiry 1½ foot flower stems produced in winter or early spring. The delightfully fragrant flowers are borne on the upper side of the spike, and come in a wide range of colors.

CULTURE: Plant in fall and early winter, 6 to a 5 inch pot, barely cover-ing the tips with a well-drained potting medium. Store in a cold frame or other cool (40° F.) place for about 4 weeks, then move to a sunny location and grow at a night temperature of 50° F., watering freely once plants start active growth. Will flower in 10-12 weeks from starting. Withhold water after flowering and store corms dry over summer.

Fritillaria imperialis   *Galanthus*

Fritillaria species   Imbricate Bulb
Liliaceae, Europe, Asia Minor, West North America and   Zone 3
        North Africa

USES: Garden, Rock Garden

HABIT: Spring blooming bulbous plants of widely diverse appearance, closely allied to *Lilium,* the genus of the true lilies. *F. imperialis* (Crown-Imperial) produces 2½-4 foot stems topped by a rosette of green leaves under which hang clusters of orange, red or yellow flowers. Both bulbs and plants have a distinctive musky odor, reminiscent of a skunk. *F. Meleagris* (Guinea Hen Flower, Chequered Lily), grows 12 inches tall and has single nodding flowers checkered purple and white. *F. persica,* from Iran, has violet-blue blossoms on 3 foot plants.

CULTURE: Plant as early in fall as possible, as bulbs tend to lose their viability as the season progresses. Plant *F. Meleagris* in masses, 3-4 inches deep and about 4 inches apart in a somewhat moist soil in partial shade. *F. imperialis* and *F. persica* require a rather porous, thoroughly drained soil and, although larger, should be planted at the same depth. Enrichment with humus and the addition of lime to the soil at the time of planting is beneficial, as is a top dressing of fertilizer. Water deeply during active growth.

Galanthus species   SNOWDROP   Bulb
Amaryllidaceae, Europe and Asia Minor   Zones 3-9

USES: Garden, Naturalizing, Rock Garden

HABIT: Small, nodding bell-shaped flowers, pleasantly fragrant and among the earliest of bulbous plants to bloom. (January to March). Two species are the most readily available and widely grown. The first is *G. nivalis,* about 4 inches tall, with white flowers marked in green. Variants include a double form, some with more green in the flower, some yellow, marked and some larger flowered kinds. *G. Elwesii* is the second, and has larger white flowers marked with green. Less frequently available are *G. byzantinus,* believed by some to be a natural hybrid, which grows to about 6 inches and is white with green markings, and *G. plicatus,* so named because the leaves are folded when first emerging. They have white flowers prominently marked with green.

CULTURE: Culture varies with the species, but all should be planted in fall 3-4 inches deep and about the same distance apart. *G. nivalis* prefers a moist, somewhat shaded location; the others do better in a dry, sunny site while all do best under cool conditions. Do not fertilize.

Galax   Geranium tuberosum

Galax urceolata   WAND-FLOWER, COLTSFOOT   Rhizome
Diapensiaceae, Eastern North America   Zone 5

USES: Rock Garden, Naturalizing, Ground Cover, Cutting (foliage)

HABIT: Evergreen round to heart-shaped leaves with toothed edges, often turning purplish or bronze in fall. 5-parted white flowers appear in 18 inch racemes in late spring and summer. A mat-forming ground cover, particularly attractive under azaleas and rhododendrons. Also improperly known as *G. rotundifolia* or *G. aphylla.*

CULTURE: Grow in rich, moist, very acid soil in full or partial shade. Under such conditions, it will colonize rapidly.

NOTE: In addition to its value as a shady ground cover, *Galax* has considerable commercial value in the florist's trade for its bold, attractive foliage.

Geranium tuberosum   Tuber
Geraniaceae, Southern Europe   Zone 5

USES: Border, Rock Garden

HABIT: Perennial to 15 inches with thick, attractive, pinnately compound basal leaves. Flowers, rose-purple to violet appear in May and are long-lasting.

CULTURE: Plant 2-3 inches deep, in an extra well-drained soil of gritty nature but enriched with organic mater. A situation in full sun is required. Keep cultivated, watered and feed every month with a balanced fertilizer. For best results, allow clumps to remain undisturbed.

Gladiolus

Gladiolus species and hybrids   Corm
Iridaceae, Tropical and South Africa, Europe,   Zone 8
Mediterranean and the Near East

USES: Garden, Cutting

HABIT: Plants with sword-shaped leaves and flower spikes to 5 feet in height, bearing numerous florets, each measuring 1-5 inches across. Bloom occurs in summer and fall, depending on when planted. Gladiolus are among the most important of cut flowers, both for the commercial grower and for the home gardener, by virtue of their size, variety of color, and keeping quality. The Garden Gladiolus, *G. x hortulanus,* was developed by intercrossing numerous species and has evolved, throughout the years, to include a tremendous range of colors, sizes and forms. *G. primulinus,* a small, hooded flower from tropical Africa, has been used to produce some miniature forms widely popular for arrangements. *G. tristis,* a species with small, fragrant flowers in white or yellow, marked with purple, is of considerable interest as a winter greenhouse subject, or in pots. *G. byzantinus,* a species from the Mediterranean Region, occurs in purple, red or white forms and is appreciably hardier than most others.

CULTURE: Plant in sun, in a well-drained, fertile soil, setting 4-6 inches deep and 6 inches apart. Fertilize with 5-10-5 at planting time, and again as flower spikes develop. Keep well-watered. To provide a succession of bloom, make staggered plantings at 2 week intervals, starting when danger of frost is past and continuing through mid-July. Staking is desirable. While gladiolus may winter over in southern areas, they are best dug when foliage yellows. Allow to dry in the sun, remove dead foliage, discard the old, spent corm and store the new ones dry at 40-50° F. over winter.

Gloriosa *Habranthus*

Gloriosa species GLORIOSA or CLIMBING LILY Tuber
Liliaceae, Africa and Asia Zone 10

USES: Pots, Cutting

HABIT: Vining plants, 3-8 feet tall bearing 4 inch, lily-like flowers with recurved and twisted narrow tepals. The species most often offered are *G. Rothschildiana,* with crimson flowers marked with yellow and sometimes white, and *G. superba,* a slightly smaller flower of yellow, changing to red. Other species include *G. Carsonii,* a purple-red with yellow center and *G. simplex,* a greenish bloom that gradually changes to yellow and red.

CULTURE: When red "eye" appears on tuber, plant individual tubers horizontally in 6 inch pots, covering with 2-4 inches of a well-drained potting mix. Keep well-watered and grow at 60-65° F., in a sunny location. Provide support for the vine which climbs by means of its tendril-like leaf tips. Keep humidity high by misting or setting the pot on a pebble-and-water tray. After flowering, reduce water to induce dormancy. Dig up tuber, divide carefully to avoid breaking and store in dry wood shavings at 60° F. until "eye" appears. Two periods of bloom per year are often possible.

NOTE: Flowers are of some importance in the florist's trade, both as a cut flower and as a long-lasting corsage bloom.

Habranthus species RAIN LILY Bulb
Amaryllidaceae, The Americas Zone 9

USES: Border, Rock Garden, Pots

HABIT: Numerous species of plants with strap-like leaves and trumpet-shaped or tubular flowers borne in summer and fall. Species include: *H. Andersonii* with yellow flowers, veined red on 6 inch stems, *H. brachy-andrus,* pink and red-purple flowers 12 inches tall, *H. gracilifolius,* green and purple flowers, 18 inches tall, *H. juncifolius,* white flowers marked with pink, green and red, *H. texanus,* yellow flowers striped with purple, 8 inches tall, and *H. tubispathus,* with flaring rose-red blooms, 9 inches tall.

CULTURE: Outdoors, plant in spring, 4-6 inches deep, in a sunny location and well-drained, sandy soil enriched with organic matter. Keep moist during the growing season, then, after flowering, withhold water to induce dormancy. In severe climates, dig in fall and store until the following spring at 60° F.

Haemanthus   Hedychium

To grow in pots, set bulbs 2-3 inches deep in a rich, loamy mixture. Grow at 50° F. night temperature, keeping moist while in active growth. Apply dilute soluble plant food every 2 weeks. After flowering, withhold water and store dormant bulbs in a cool area over winter, restarting the cycle in spring.

Haemanthus species   BLOOD LILY   Bulb
Amaryllidaceae, South and Tropical Africa   Zone 10

USES: Pots

HABIT: Broad basal leaves subtend a dense terminal umbel of spidery flowers in red, pink or white. The most commonly offered species, *H. Katharinae* produces umbels up to 9 inches across in bright red, *H. multiflorus,* clusters to 6 inches of deep red, *H. albiflos,* 2 inch white heads.

CULTURE: In late winter or early spring, set bulbs with tip just above the surface of the well-drained potting mixture. *Haemanthus* bloom best when potbound, so select a pot that will give about 1 inch of clearance all around the circumference of the bulb. Keep moist during growth and feed about once a month with a soluble plant food. Grow in a sunny location. While many recommend a night temperature of 55° F., we have found that *Haemanthus* will perform well at normal household night temperatures of 65° F. May be grown outdoors when night temperatures do not drop below 50° F. In fall, when foliage starts to die back, withhold water to induce dormancy and store in pot. Start cycle again in late winter or early spring.

Hedychium species   GINGER LILY   Rhizome
Zingiberaceae, Tropical Asia and The Himalayas   Zones 8-9

USES: Containers, Border

HABIT: 4-7 foot plants with glossy lance-shaped leaves and long, slender stems bearing terminal spikes of showy flowers in white, yellow, orange or red, often delightfully fragrant. Of the more commonly grown species, *H. coccineum* is bright red, *H. coronarium* white, and *H. flavescens* yellow.

CULTURE: Plant in early spring in a standard potting mixture and supply ample water at all times while in active growth. So great is the need for water that it may be a good idea to have the pot or container standing in water. Plants may be set outdoors, protected from full sun, when temperatures remain consistently above 50° F. at night. After plants have finished flowering, gradually reduce water and keep soil almost dry throughout the winter, starting up again in spring.

Helianthus tuberosus

Helianthus tuberosus

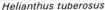

Helianthus tuberosus   JERUSALEM ARTICHOKE   Tuber
Compositae, Eastern and Central North America   Zone 4

USES: Food Crop, Possibly as Garden Screen.

HABIT: A vigorous member of the Sunflower family, growing to as much as 12 feet in height with 8 inch toothed leaves and 3½ inch disc flowers that appear atop rigid, upright stems in late summer and early fall.

CULTURE: Cut tubers into pieces containing one or more eyes. About the date of the last spring frost, plant 6 inches deep and 2 feet apart in any soil, preferably one of fairly low fertility to discourage rampant top growth at the expense of tuber production. Keep well-watered. After frost, dig tubers and store in a cool location in sand or similar inert material.

NOTE: Jerusalem Artichokes are quite aggressive and, once planted, almost impossible to eradicate. For this reason, it is wise when planting, to devote a separate part of the garden to them, alone.

Jerusalem Artichokes may be eaten boiled as a starchy vegetable, or made into delicious pickles. Here's a fine old Southern pickle recipe:

ARTICHOKE PICKLES

½ peck artichokes
1 bunch celery
1 cauliflower
10 bell peppers
   (½ green, ½ red for color)
1½ qts. vinegar
3 cups salt

1 pt. water
1 cup flour
½ cup dry English mustard
3 cups sugar

1-1½ Tbs. turmeric

Cut up vegetables and soak overnight in a brine solution made up of the 3 cups of salt and as much water as necessary to dissolve it and cover the vegetables. Drain and set aside. Mix together the flour, mustard, sugar and turmeric and make a paste of them, using some of the vinegar. Bring the remaining vinegar and the water to a boil, add the paste and the vegetables and bring once more to a boil. Put in sterilized jars and seal.

Helleborus

Hemerocallis

Helleborus species   CHRISTMAS ROSE,   Tuberous Root
LENTEN ROSE

Ranunculaceae, Europe and Asia   Zone 3

USES: Border, Underplanting for Foundation Plantings

HABIT: Plants with evergreen, palmately compound leaves and single-petaled flowers, white, pink, red, green, purple or brown, borne in winter or early spring. Most reach a height of about 1 foot. *H. niger* (Christmas Rose) is white, sometimes flushed with green and pink and blooms in late winter. *H. orientalis* (Lenten Rose) blooms in early spring with flowers cream fading to brown. Reddish-purple forms are available.

CULTURE: Grow in a deep, rich, highly organic soil well-supplied with moisture. Provide at least partial shade and mulch to conserve moisture.

NOTE: Plant parts of the various *Helleborus* species are toxic.

Hemerocallis species and cultivars   DAYLILY   Tuberous Root,
Rhizome

Liliaceae, Central Europe to China and Japan   Zone 3

USES: Border, Naturalizing

HABIT: Plants up to 3 feet in height with rather grass-like foliage and bearing lily-like flowers in various shades of yellow, pink, orange, red or purple or combinations of those colors, variously from May through September. The individual flowers are ephemeral, lasting only a day, but flowers are produced in many-budded scapes, so the result is a long period of bloom. Some cultivars and species are fragrant. Both evergreen and deciduous types are found, the latter generally hardier. *Hemerocallis* have become a favorite of hobbyists and plant hybridizers, with literally thousands of cultivars, including tetraploid and double forms now widely available. The species *H. fulva* (Orange Daylily) is familiar to all, having escaped to grow wild by the roadside, while *H. minor,* an early blooming, dwarf, fragrant, yellow flowering plant is much used as a parent in producing dwarf strains.

CULTURE: Daylilies are among the easiest of all garden plants to grow. They will flourish under a wide range of conditions, from full sun to almost complete shade, from dry soils to those that are so moist as to preclude growing most other plants. For best results, a good garden loam

Hermodactylus

Hippeastrum hybrid

and full sun are recommended. Plant in either fall or spring, to the depth at which they previously grew. Apply balanced fertilizer during the growing season and provide ample moisture.

NOTE: Dried flowers of *Hemerocallis* are a fairly important food source in the Orient. New tuberous roots are also edible.

| **Hermodactylus tuberosus** | SNAKE'S HEAD IRIS | Tuber |
| *Iridaceae,* Southern France and the Mediterranean Region | | Zone 5 |

USES: Border, Naturalizing

HABIT: Often referred to as *Iris tuberosus,* this Mediterranean native grows to about 18 inches in height and has become naturalized throughout portions of the British Isles. The falls, much larger than the green standards, are plum purple, velvety in texture and without a beard.

CULTURE: Plant about 3-4 inches deep in a sunny location, selecting a well-drained soil, preferably of neutral or slightly alkaline reaction.

| **Hippeastrum hybrids** | AMARYLLIS | Bulb |
| *Amaryllidaceae,* Tropical America | | Zone 9 |

USES: Pots, Garden (in deep South)

HABIT: This is the "Amaryllis" of house plant fame. Large, trumpet-shaped flowers as much as 8 inches across are borne in clusters (usually of 4) atop 1-2 foot leafless hollow stems. Colors include shades of red, orange, yellow, green, brown and pink, as well as white and striped kinds. The 18-24 inch strap-shaped leaves usually appear after flowering.

CULTURE: In the garden, plant in a well-drained, sunny location, covering the bulbs with 2-3 inches of soil. Withhold water in early fall to induce dormancy, then cover with a winter mulch.

To grow in pots, plant in winter, selecting a pot 2 inches larger in diameter than the bulb. Set bulb with its upper half above the surface of the well-drained potting mixture. Grow in a warm, sunny location (gentle bottom heat is beneficial), water sparingly until growth starts and then liberally once in active growth. Foliage will usually appear after blooming. Keep leaves growing after blooming, either in the house or by plunging the pot in a sunny location in the garden, regularly applying a soluble plant food. In September, withhold water to induce dormancy, bring in pot if outside, and store pot on its side for 2-3 months, after which cycle can be begun again.

Hippeastrum Evansiae

Hippeastrum Calyptrata

H. Calyptrata

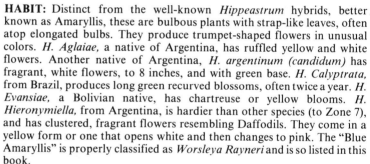

Hippeastrum species   Bulb
Amaryllidaceae, Tropical America

USES: Pots

HABIT: Distinct from the well-known *Hippeastrum* hybrids, better known as Amaryllis, these are bulbous plants with strap-like leaves, often atop elongated bulbs. They produce trumpet-shaped flowers in unusual colors. *H. Aglaiae,* a native of Argentina, has ruffled yellow and white flowers. Another native of Argentina, *H. argentinum (candidum)* has fragrant, white flowers, to 8 inches, and with green base. *H. Calyptrata,* from Brazil, produces long green recurved blossoms, often twice a year. *H. Evansiae,* a Bolivian native, has chartreuse or yellow blooms. *H. Hieronymiella,* from Argentina, is hardier than other species (to Zone 7), and has clustered, fragrant flowers resembling Daffodils. They come in a yellow form or one that opens white and then changes to pink. The "Blue Amaryllis" is properly classified as *Worsleya Rayneri* and is so listed in this book.

CULTURE: In general, select a pot twice the size of the bulb and pot in a well-drained mixture consisting of 1/3 peat or sphagnum, 1/3 sand and 1/3 loam. Use pieces of broken pot in the bottom to provide good drainage. Set with 1/3 to 1/2 of the bulb below the soil line (exceptions appear below), water, and keep in a cool dark place without additional watering until growth starts. After sprouting occurs, bring to a warm, sunny location and resume watering. Fertilize once a month with soluble plant food. After flowering finishes, allow leaves to ripen and then withhold water during the dormant period (usually October through December). *H. Calyptrata,* which in nature grows epiphytically on trees, should be planted in a 6-8 inch pot with just the bulb base covered. It should be watered only once a week in hot weather and every two weeks in cooler weather, making sure that no water gets on the leaves or bulb. Grow in full sun except during July to September, when filtered light is required. *H. argentinum* should be planted with just the tip of the bulb exposed. *H. Hieronymiella* should be planted with bulbs covered with 4-5 inches of soil. For this reason, a large tub or very deep pot is required. It can also be grown outdoors in Zone 7-10, in a very well-drained situation. In all cases, the genus seems to prefer being potbound, so keep growing in the same pot for several years, until production of offset bulbs makes this no longer possible.

Homeria

Hosta

Homeria species Corm
Iridaceae, South Africa

USES: Pots, Cutting

HABIT: Summer-blooming plants with linear leaves and bell-shaped flowers of six segments that open flat and close at night. *H. Breyniana (collina)* has fragrant pink or yellow flowers; the blooms of *H. lilacina* are lavender veined with purple and a yellow and purple base blotch; *H. ochroleuca* is yellow, with or without pink markings.

CULTURE: Plant in a well-drained, rather peaty medium and grow under filtered light at a temperature of 65° F. night. Keep evenly moist during active growth. Homerias go dormant during fall and should be stored dry and warm until growth starts again.

HOSTA species, FUNKIA, PLANTAIN LILY Rhizome
Liliaceae, Japan, China, and Korea Zone 3

USES: The bold foliage and dependable flowering make this genus invaluable for the border, for edging and for plantings in partial shade.

HABIT: Clump-forming perennials with large, basal leaves and tall racemes of white, purple or blue flowers borne well above the foliage in late summer or fall. *H. elata,* the tallest of the species in widespread cultivation, may reach a height of 5 feet, with large broad green leaves and lavender flowers. *H. Fortunei* is a compact grower, 1½-2 feet, with lilac or purple flowers. Varieties with white or yellow-variegated leaves are available. *H. lancifolia* has slender glossy green leaves and lavender flowers and is especially effective in mass plantings. *H. plantaginea (subcordata)* is the most fragrant of all with large glossy green leaves and large white flowers. *S. Sieboldiana* has very broad bluish leaves and white or lavender blooms. *H. undulata* is distinguished by having undulate or wavy foliage striped with white or cream. The lilac flowers are borne earlier than most other species. *H. ventricosa (caerulea)* has deep green leaves and dark violet flowers.

CULTURE: Widely tolerant of different soils and growing conditions, *Hostas* perform best when grown in a fertile moist soil. The blue-leaved forms attain their best color in sun, variegated forms require the most shade. Shade requirements increase the further south they are grown. Water during periods of drought.

73

Hyacinthus orientalis

Hyacinthus orientalis albulus

Hyacinthus orientalis

Legend has it that this fragrant garden subject was named for Hyacinthus, a handsome mortal youth, beloved of Apollo and also of Zephyrus. The latter, jealous of Hyacinthus' apparent preference for Apollo, interfered when the two were playing at discus. He caused a strong wind to arise which diverted a discus so that it struck Hyacinthus in the head, fatally wounding him. From the blood, Apollo caused fragrant purple flowers to spring up.

Long grown in the Middle East, and mentioned in the works of Hafiz and other Persian poets, Hyacinths were introduced to Europe from the eastern Mediterranean in 1562, through Padua, and thence to Holland. Although Hyacinths were first grown in Europe in the Sixteenth Century, interest in them peaked in the Eighteenth Century, when many hundreds of varieties were bred, not only in Holland, but in France and Germany as well.

Hyacinthus orientalis   HYACINTH   Bulb
Liliaceae, Mediterranean Europe, Syria and Asia Minor   Zone 4

USES: Gardens, Cutting, Forcing in Pots or Glasses

HABIT: 8-12 inch plants bearing clusters of bell-shaped, extremely fragrant flowers in April and May. Colors include white, pale yellow, pink, red, blue, lavender and orange. Many cultivars of both single and double flowered forms are available in the trade. The variety *H. orientalis albulus,* known as the French Roman Hyacinth, produces flowers in less dense spikes in shades of pink or blue as well as white, but it is generally less hardy.

CULTURE: In the garden, plant 4-6 inches deep and 6-8 inches apart, in a sunny location with well-drained garden soil. Bulbs should be set out in the fall, after flowering. Allow foliage to turn yellow before cutting back.

For forcing, obtain the largest possible bulbs, and plant in a standard, well-drained medium, covering with about 1 inch of soil. Use 5 bulbs to a 6 inch pot. Water; then set the pot in a cold frame and expose to at least 6 weeks of near-freezing temperature. (Specially precooled bulbs can be obtained, thus eliminating this step). Bring the pots to a sunny window with a night temperature of 50-55° F.

Hyacinths can also easily be grown in glasses especially manufactured for the purpose. Using a prepared bulb, scrape the base of the bulb with a knife to remove old roots. Fill the glass with water, setting the bulb in the glass with the base just touching the surface of the water. A piece of charcoal in the water will prevent the possibility of foul water. Keep in a cool dark place while roots are growing with a cone of construction paper over the top of the bulb to encourage lengthening of the stem so that flowering will not occur down in the neck of the bulb. When roots fill the glass, bring to the light and grow at a night temperature of 50-55° F.

NOTE: Hyacinths tend to be rather formal in their appearance, particularly those from the larger bulbs. After a year or so, however, the bulbs tend to break up, the spikes become less dense and more graceful.

Hymenocallis

Incarvillea

Hymenocallis species ISMENE, PERUVIAN DAFFODIL Bulb
Amaryllidaceae, The Americas Zone 8

USES: Border, Pots

HABIT: Plants with strap-shaped leaves and leafless stalks produced in summer and bearing 3-5½ inch, fragrant flowers in white or shades of yellow. *H. narcissiflora (Ismene calathina)* grows to 2 feet with white flowers. A pale yellow cultivar is also available. *H. x festalis* has white flowers with shorter perianth tubes than the above. *H. caroliniana* grows wild throughout the Southeast, with fragrant white flowers on 18 inch stems. *H. Amancaes* has bright yellow blooms on 2 foot plants.

CULTURE: In the garden, plant in spring, 3-5 inches deep and 12 inches apart, in a well-drained soil high in organic content. Full sun or light shade suits them well. In areas above their limit of hardiness, dig prior to frost, allow foliage to wither, then store in dry vermiculite or peat at a temperature of 70° F. Storage at cooler temperatures will prevent bulbs from producing flowers the following year.

In pots, set in a regular potting mixture to which has been added a small quantity of ground limestone. Keep moist and feed monthly with a soluble plant food. May be set outdoors after night temperatures exceed 60° F.

Incarvillea Delavayi HARDY GLOXINIA Tuberous Root
Bignoniaceae, China Zone 6

USES: Garden, Rock Garden

HABIT: 2 foot plants with pinnately compound leaves and 18-24 inch racemes of funnel-shaped flowers, purple with yellow throat. Blooms in May and June.

CULTURE: Plant in spring in a sunny location, choosing a rich, highly fertile acid soil. Cover with 2 inches of soil, setting 12-15 inches apart. Water well and keep moderately moist throughout the season until after blooming ceases. To promote flowering, remove faded flowers. Foliage dies back after frost, but cycle will repeat the following year.

Ipheion

Ipomoea Batatas

Ipheion uniflorum   Bulb
Amaryllidaceae, South America   Zone 6

USES: Garden, Naturalizing, Pots

HABIT: Pale blue flowers with white eyes, borne 1 to a 6 inch stem during late spring. The grassy foliage rarely stands more than a few inches high and dies back shortly after flowering. Increases rapidly in warmer areas, hence it is excellent for mass plantings.

CULTURE: In the garden, plant in early fall in a sunny location, 3 inches deep and the same distance apart. A well-drained soil will produce best results. In the northern part of its range, apply a winter mulch.

To grow indoors, plant 1 inch deep in a standard potting mixture; grow at a night temperature of 60° F., keeping moist when in growth and until foliage withers in late spring. Then dry off, separate and replant in fall.

Ipomoea Batatas   SWEET POTATO   Tuberous Root
Convolvulaceae, Tropical Regions   Zone 7

USES: Major Food Crop, Ornamental Hanging Baskets

HABIT: Low-growing, vining perennial with entire or lobed leaves and rooting along the stems. Flowers vary from pink to rose-purple. Produces edible tuberous roots in various colors and divided into two types, dry-fleshed and moist-fleshed (the latter often erroneously called "yams" which appellation is properly applied to species of Dioscorea). Numerous cultivars, varying in color, size, leaf-shape and growth habit are available.

CULTURE: Using "seed potatoes", plant tubers in a hot-bed and cover with 3-4 inches of soil. Keep moist, and when sprouts reach 8 inches in height, pull (do not cut) them from the tuber and plant in the garden. (This step can be eliminated by buying started plants.) Set out after nights are uniformly warm (at least 60° F.) 12-15 inches apart and 4 inches deep in an acid, well-drained light sandy loam. Avoid poorly-drained or heavy soils. Soils of relatively low fertility produce best results; do not fertilize after planting. At harvest time, take care not to bruise the tender skin. To cure, let dry 2-3 hours, avoiding exposure to sun, then store in baskets lined with newspaper in a humid atmosphere at a temperature of 80-85° F. Such curing will improve flavor and add to keeping qualities. Sweet potatoes may be cooked in a number of ways: candied, baked, fried, French-fried, mashed and baked in a casserole with marshmallows or even as a pie, similar to pumpkin.

Iris x germanica

Iris

The genus *Iris* is a proper subject for several volumes in itself, so discussion here will necessarily be limited to those species most commonly grown.

Iris are not without their place in history and legend. Thought to be of medicinal value, they were imported into Egypt from Syria (somewhere) around 1450 B. C. While the medicinal value never was established, Iris root (orrisroot) continued to be used for millenia as a breath-sweetener and perfume for linens, and beads of it were fashioned into necklaces which were thought to have magical, disease-preventative properties. Production of the fragrant orris centered in Italy and France, and was a major commercial venture. Today some use is still made of the product in cosmetics and dentifrices. Orris is derived from *I. florentina.*

Flowers now identified as *Iris* (probably *I. Pseudacorus*) appeared in heraldry as early as the Fifth Century A. D. as the emblem of Frankish and later French kings. Gradually the symbols evolved to the stylized "Fleur-de-lis", which despite its name, is an Iris, not a lily.

For purposes of simplicity, *Iris* can be divided into *I. bulbous* and *I. non-bulbous* or rhizomatous types, and the latter, in turn, into Bearded, Crested and Beardless forms.

CULTURE: Easily grown. Plant 3 inches deep and about 4 inches apart in a sunny, well-drained soil, preferably on the gritty side.

Iris x germanica   TALL BEARDED IRIS   Rhizome
Iridaceae, Central and Southern Europe   Zone 4

USES: Borders

HABIT: Plants with sword-shaped leaves, blooming in late spring and producing large, often fragrant flowers in virtually all colors of the rainbow. The name *I. x germanica* is of dubious authenticity, since the full parentage of these Iris is not known. So widely are they grown, and so much interest has arisen in them, that they have become a favorite subject of the plant breeder, with literally thousands of cultivars introduced. The flowers are large, with three upright petals, the "standards", and three drooping sepals, the "falls", the latter decorated in the central portion with the "beard" which may be of the same or a different color as the falls. Plants grow 2 to 3½ feet in height and bloom in an infinite range of colors and color combinations. Some success has been achieved in developing cultivars that rebloom in the fall.

CULTURE: Plant rhizomes in late summer, even with the surface of the soil, with the feeder roots covered, in a sunny location and a limy, well-drained soil. Set rhizomes about 1 foot apart to allow for natural increase. Plants will tolerate drought conditions. Spray to control Iris Borer, a major source of problems, and remove dead foliage. Planting is best done in late summer.

Iris pumila   *Iris cristata*

Iris pumila   Rhizome
Iridaceae, Central Europe and Asia Minor   Zone 4

USES: Border, Rock Garden

HABIT: Plants to less than a foot in height, with sword-shaped leaves and flowers in purple, wine, yellow, or cream, with variously colored beards. Blooms appear in early spring, about April in the northeast United States.

CULTURE: Plant rhizomes even with the surface of the soil, with the feeder roots covered, in a sunny location and a limy, well-drained soil. Set rhizomes about 1 foot apart to allow for natural increase. Plants will tolerate drought conditions. Spray to control Iris Borer, a major source of problems, and remove dead foliage. Planting is best done in late summer.

Iris cristata   Rhizome
Iridaceae, Northeastern United States   Zone 5

USES: Border, Rock Garden

HABIT: Plants to about 6 inches in height with upright, sword-shaped leaves that die back to the ground in early autumn. The flowers, borne in May and June, are typically lavender, but white and purple forms are found. Crests are usually white or yellow.

CULTURE: Plant about 8 inches apart in fall or spring, with the top portion of the rhizome above the surface of the soil. If planted too deeply, rotting will occur. Plant in a very well-drained, somewhat alkaline soil, in sun, or better yet, partial shade.

Iris tectorum   Iris Kaempferi

Iris tectorum   JAPANESE ROOF IRIS   Rhizome
Iridaceae, China   Zone 5

USES: Border, Ground Cover

HABIT: Used in Japan to bind thatched roofs, this 18 inch plant has evergreen, sword-shaped leaves and 6 inch flowers typically of lavender with crinkled falls striped with darker purple and crested in white or yellow. A white form is also available in the trade.

CULTURE: Plant in fertile, well-drained soil, somewhat on the alkaline side, and grow in full sun, keeping quite dry. Will multiply rapidly, forming an excellent and unusual ground cover.

Among the beardless Iris are included:

Iris Kaempferi   JAPANESE or ORIENTAL   Rhizome
    ORCHID IRIS
Iridaceae, Japan   Zone 5

USES: Borders, Waterside Plantings

HABIT: Late June- and early July-blooming plants, growing to about 2 feet in height. The flowers are large, rather flattened, often with prominently colored veining, and are available in a number of colors including wine, purple, lavender, blue and white, often with contrasting markings in the throat. Double forms are also in the trade.

CULTURE: Plant in sun or partial shade, in a rich, moisture-retentive soil, highly enriched with organic matter and free of lime.

Iris Pseudacorus   *Iris sibirica*

Iris Pseudacorus   YELLOW FLAG   Rhizome
Iridaceae, Western Europe and North Africa   Zone 4

USES: Waterside or Marsh Plantings, Border

HABIT: This is the Yellow Flag that has naturalized along streams throughout many parts of the country. It grows to about 5 feet in height and bears bright yellow flowers in early summer. A form with variegated foliage is known.

CULTURE: While native to wet places and excellent to grow in them, *I. Pseudacorus* can also be grown in the border, as long as ample moisture is provided. Soil should be highly organic and of acid reaction.

Iris sibirica   SIBERIAN IRIS   Rhizome
Iridaceae, Central Europe to Russia   Zone 3

USES: Borders, Naturalizing

HABIT: Two to three-foot plants with narrow, grassy foliage and flowers in shades of purple, blue, wine and white borne in June. Falls are marked with white or yellow veining. Extremely graceful in their appearance; a natural combination with early-blooming Hemerocallis.

CULTURE: Easily grown in almost any soil or location, but will flower best and spread most rapidly in a moist, sunny situation with acid soil. Plant about 18 inches apart.

Iris spuria   *Iris reticulata (top)   Iris Danfordiae (bottom)*

Iris spuria   BUTTERFLY IRIS   Rhizome
Iridaceae, Central and Southern Europe, The Levant   Zone 3

USES: Border

HABIT: Plants with linear, or sometimes sword-shaped leaves, growing 3 to 5 feet in height and blooming in early summer. Typically lavender, but the color is variable and includes pale blues and yellow-throated types.

CULTURE: Easily grown in a sunny situation and well-drained soil. Plant about 1 foot apart.

The bulbous Irises include those of the so-called Reticulata Group, with bulbs heavily netted. Among the group are:

Iris reticulata   Bulb
Iridaceae, Caucasus and Asia Minor   Zone 3

USES: Border, Rock Garden

HABIT: Plants that bloom at about 8 inches in height, then foliage grows to about 18 inches. Blooming in March, the flowers are typically deep violet-purple marked with orange, but blue, reddish and white forms are known. Fragrant.

Iris Danfordiae   Bulb
Iridaceae, Eastern Asia Minor   Zone 4

USES: Border, Rock Garden

HABIT: Plants to 1 foot in height with blue-green leaves and practically standardless flowers in yellow, spotted with olive-green and marked with orange. Blooms in March.

CULTURE: As for *I. reticulata,* but slightly less hardy.

Iris Bakerana

Iris Bakerana   Bulb
Iridaceae, Asia Minor   Zone 4

USES: Border, Rock Garden

HABIT: A very early-blooming species that may bloom in February in the New York area, with violet flowers, marked with white or yellow in the throat. Fragrant. 1 foot tall.

CULTURE: As for *I. reticulata,* but plant in protected location or mulch at the northern extreme of its range.

Iris histrioides   Bulb
Iridaceae, Asia Minor   Zone 4

USES: Border, Rock Garden

HABIT: Nine-inch plants with bright blue or occasionally purple-blue flowers, marked in the center with white and yellow. Very early blooming. Rather stiff flowers appear with the flowers.

CULTURE: As for *I. Danfordiae.*

Among the taller bulbous Iris are two which are of major importance in the garden.

Iris xiphioides   ENGLISH IRIS   Bulb
Iridaceae, Pyrenees Mountains   Zone 6

USES: Border

HABIT: 18 inch plants, blooming in June and July. The large flowers with rounded standards are typically blue-purple marked with yellow, but lavender and mahogany-red cultivars are available.

CULTURE: Plant 3-4 inches deep and 4-6 inches apart, in a sunny location and a soil high in humus content and of acid reaction. Ample moisture should be present, and supplemental watering during dry summer months is advised. A winter mulch in areas near the northern limits of its hardiness is beneficial.

Dutch Iris

CULTURE: Plant 3-4 inches deep and 4-6 inches apart, in a sunny location and a soil high in humus content and of acid reaction. Ample moisture should be present, and supplemental watering during dry summer months is advised. A winter mulch in areas near the northern limits of its hardiness is beneficial.

Iris Xiphium   SPANISH IRIS   Bulb
Iridaceae, Southern France and Iberian Peninsula   Zone 5

USES: Border, Cutting, Forcing

HABIT: Blooming in June, these 2 foot plants have narrow leaves and 4 inch flowers with rather thin segments. Typically, flowers are blue or blue-violet, marked with a yellow or orange blotch on the falls. Of infinitely more importance are the Dutch Iris, a product of crosses between *I. Xiphium* and various other species including *I. tingitana.* These come in various shades of blue and purple, as well as white, all usually with the characteristic blotch, are widely grown in the garden and are a major florist's cut-flower crop when forced.

CULTURE: In the garden, plant 3-4 inches deep and 4-6 inches apart, selecting a sunny site and a well-drained soil. Mulch toward the northern limits of its hardiness.

FORCING: Commercial growers start with bulbs that have been specially treated by curing for 10 days at 90 degrees temperature. If such are not available to you, store bulbs at or near 90° for 10 days to two weeks. Plant in fairly deep pots, just covering the tips of the bulbs with the planting medium, which should be a standard, well-drained one. Water and precool under conditions where temperatures will approximate 48 degrees for 4-8 weeks, then grow under night temperatures of 50-55° F., providing ample sun and moisture.

Ixia

Ixiolirion

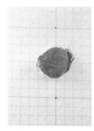

Ixia species and hybrids   CORN LILY   Corm
Iridaceae, South Africa   Zone 8

USES: Gardens, Cutting, Pots

HABIT: 6-36 inch plants with grass-like foliage surrounding slender spikes, which bear 2 inch star-shaped flowers in shades of blue, purple, red, pink, orange, yellow, green or white. Many have darker centers. Outdoors they bloom in late spring and early summer; the foliage dies back in mid-summer. Species include: *I. azurea,* pale blue with darker blotch; *I. campanulata,* purple or crimson; *I. leucantha,* white, or in a variant, yellow; *I. maculata,* white or yellow with darker blotch; *I. monadelpha,* lilac, red or yellow; and *I. viridiflora,* green with dark center.

CULTURE: In the garden, plant in fall, in areas where hardy (Zones 8-10); otherwise, in spring. Plant 4 inches deep and 3-4 inches apart in a sunny location with an extra well-drained, gritty soil, which will remain dry in summer. Summer moisture will cause plants to die out after a couple of years. Apply a mulch of 3 inches of organic matter in spring. Feed regularly with a 5-10-5 fertilizer every 2 weeks after the leaves appear. After flowering, lift, dry in an airy place, cut off dead foliage and store dry and cool (50° F.).

To force, plant 5 or 6 corms to a 6 inch pot, covering with 1 inch of well-drained potting medium. Start in the cold frame for 4-6 weeks, then move to a sunny location at 55° F. night temperature.

Ixiolirion tataricum   LILY-OF-THE-ALTAI   Bulb
Amaryllidaceae, Asia   Zone 7

USES: Garden, Cutting

HABIT: 12-16 inch plants with narrow, grass-like foliage and slender stems produced in late spring or early summer bearing clusters of lightly fragrant, soft blue flowers.

CULTURE: Where hardy (Zones 7-10) plant in fall in a well-drained, gritty soil, in full sun. Mulch in early spring and provide ample moisture during the growing season, but do not fertilize. Above their limit of hardiness (Zones 6 and above), plant in spring under the conditions described above, dig in fall before first frost and store over winter in dry peat or vermiculite at a temperature of 60° F.

Kaempferia　　　　　　　　　　　　　　　　*Kniphofia*

Kaempferia species　　RESURRECTION LILY,　　Rhizome
　　　　　　　　　　　　DWARF GINGER LILY
Zingiberaceae, Asia and Africa　　　　　　　　Zone 10

USES: Pots

HABIT: Plants with aromatic rhizomes, attractive foliage and rather short-lived flowers in a variety of colors. The leaves are often broadly oval and often beautifully variegated. One of the species with the most attractive variegation is *K. Roscoeana,* which has large rounded leaves of bronze variegated with silver and bears white flowers. *K. Gilbertii* has dark green leaves, sometimes with a white central stripe, and white flowers striped violet; *K. pulchra* has wide dark green leaves banded in bronze and grayish-white beneath, and lavender flowers spotted with yellow and white.

CULTURE: Plant in a well-drained, rather peaty medium and grow under filtered light at a temperature of 65° F. night. Keep evenly moist during active growth. Kaempferias go dormant during fall and should be stored dry and warm until growth starts again.

Kniphofia species and hybrids　　TRITOMA　　Rhizome
RED-HOT-POKER
Liliaceae, Madagascar, Tropical and South Africa　　Zone 4

USES: Border, Cutting

HABIT: Stout plants 1-6 feet tall with long, grassy leaves and poker-shaped flowers from July-September in shades and combinations of yellow, orange, red and cream. Most of the plants available are hybrids, probably derived from *K. Uvaria* and the earlier-blooming *K. Tuckii.*

CULTURE: Grow in full sun in a sandy, well-drained soil. Provide winter mulch. In areas where not hardy, lift roots in fall and store in dry soil at a temperature of 50° F.

Koellikeria　　　　　　　　　　　　　　　　*Ledebouria*

Koellikeria erinoides　　　　　　　　　　　　　　　　　　　　Rhizome
Gesneriaceae, Central and South America

USES: Pots

HABIT: Plants with dark green, velvety 4 inch leaves, marked with silver and somewhat resembling those of a *Sinningia.* Graceful 1 foot racemes of small deep rose red flowers with white to cream lip, borne in summer.

CULTURE: Set rhizomes on the surface of moistened milled sphagnum moss and cover with ½ inch of the same material. Keep moist and grow at 70-75° F. until growth starts. Grow under conditions of low light intensity at first, then provide increasing light. As plants attain some size, repot in 4-5 inch pots in a humusy potting medium, keep warm and moist and provide filtered or fluorescent light. After flowering is completed, gradually withhold water to promote dormancy, dig plants, divide rhizomes and start cycle anew.

Ledebouria socialis　　　　SCILLA VIOLACEAE,　　　　Bulb
　　　　　　　　　　　　　SILVER SQUILL
Liliaceae, South Africa

USES: Pots

HABIT: From glossy red bases arise clusters of beautifully colored leaves, red below and green mottled with silver above. The foliage is strap-shaped and rather fleshy and encloses slender racemes of tiny green and purple, bell-shaped flowers. Grows to 6 inches in height and rapidly forms clumps within the pot. Flowers in late winter or early spring; foliage persists for a long time.

CULTURE: A plant of the easiest culture. We recommend planting the bulb, partially exposed, in a well-drained, peaty planting medium, and growing in filtered light at a night temperature of 55-65°. Keep evenly moist, although variations in soil mix, temperature, or watering are not likely to interfere with success in growing and flowering it.

NOTE: This is a real gem for the house plant enthusiast. Few true bulbs have really attractive foliage, but that of *Ledebouria* is lovely. Even without the tiny, charming flowers, this plant would be worth growing.

Leontopodium   *Leucojum*

Leontopodium alpinum   EDELWEISS   Rhizome
Compositae, Europe   Zone 4

USES: Rock Garden, Border

HABIT: A creeping plant to about 12 inches in height, with narrow silver-gray alternate leaves and inconspicuous tiny yellow flowers during July and August, surrounded by woolly white bracts. The subject of song and legend, it spreads by means of its rhizomes, forming attractive loose tufts. An outstanding rock garden subject; one of the relatively few providing summer interest.

CULTURE: Plant in a gritty, well-drained soil, preferably of slightly alkaline reaction, spaced about 8 inches apart. Should be grown in full sun.

Leucojum species   SNOWFLAKE   Bulb
Amaryllidaceae, Europe and Western Mediterranean Region   Zone 4

USES: Border, Naturalizing, Rock Garden

HABIT: Bulbs similar to those of *Narcissus,* producing white, bell-shaped flowers, tipped with green, or more rarely, red or yellow. The two most frequently grown species are: *L. aestivum* (Summer Snowflake) which grows 9-12 inches tall and blooms in May or June with white flowers tipped with green, and *L. vernum* (Spring Snowflake), 4-12 inches tall, with fragrant flowers of the same color in March and April. Less well-known are *L. autumnale,* 9 inches, white tinged with red, blooming in August and September, and *L. nicaeense,* an early spring bloomer, 1 foot in height with white tinged with green.

CULTURE: *Leucojum* species vary significantly in their cultural requirements. All should be planted as early in the fall as possible (late-planted bulbs may not flower the first year), at a depth of about 3 inches. *L. aestivum* prefers a constantly moist soil and, at most, morning sun. Under such conditions it will naturalize rapidly. *L. vernum* prefers drier conditions, and again, only morning sun. *L. autumnale* demands perfect drainage, as does *L. nicaeense,* the latter being appreciably less hardy.

Lewisia

Liatris

Lewisia species   Tuberous Root, Corm
Portulacaceae, Western North America   Zones-Various

USES: Rock Garden, Border Foreground

HABIT: Fleshy-stemmed plants with small leaves in basal rosettes. The flowers, borne singly or in panicles, appear in spring or early summer. Many species are evergreen; in others the foliage dies back in late summer. *L. columbiana* grows to 1 foot, is evergreen, and has flowers on 2 inch scapes in rose or white; *L. Tweedyi,* perhaps the showiest of the genus, grows to 4 inches and has 2-inch bright pink flowers.

CULTURE: Requires excellent drainage. The addition of sand, gravel and peat to the soil will improve their performance. Best grown in partial shade in dry soils, can tolerate full sun under moister conditions.

NOTE: The root of *L. rediviva* provided a staple of diet for Indian tribes of the Pacific Northwest.

Liatris species   GAY-FEATHER,   Corm, Rhizome
                         SNAKEROOT   Tuberous Root
Compositae, North America   Zone 3

USES: Sunny Border, Wild Garden, Along Streams or Ponds

HABIT: Tall, narrow spikes or racemes, opening from the top down and bearing purple or occasionally white florets in summer and fall. *L. graminifolia* grows to about 4 feet, *L. pycnostachya* 3-5 feet, *L. scariosa* to 3 feet and *L. spicata* usually 3-5 feet, with dwarf cultivars available.

CULTURE: Widely tolerant as to soils. Grow in full sun, preferably in soils of low fertility and with excellent drainage. Only *L. spicata* will endure winter moisture. To prolong blooming period, trim off spent flowers.

L. Aurelian Hybrids

L. Mid-Century Hybrids

L. candidum   L. auratum

While the term "Lily" has been and is still used to describe flowers of many unrelated genera, the true lilies are members of the genus *Lilium.*

Lilies are among the oldest known cultivated flowers. *L. candidum* was portrayed on frescoes and pottery found in Crete and dating back almost 4,000 years. Bas-reliefs found at Ninevah and dating to 700 B.C. also depict lilies. The philosopher and "father of botany", Theophrastus, described them late in the Fourth Century, B.C.

While the "Lilies of the Field" (Heb. "Shushan") of the Bible were probably *Iris, Sternbergia, Anemone* or *Ornithogalum,* true lilies are mentioned in the New Testament (Gr. "Krinon"). A bulb of *L. candidum* was discovered in a tomb with an Egyptian mummy, and the species was described in numerous Greek and Roman books. Medicinal properties were ascribed to the species; it was used to make up an ointment for burns, and this usage has persisted to this day. Roman soldiers undoubtedly carried *L. candidum* across the Alps, and later, Crusaders brought the bulbs back from Palestine. *L. candidum* was also included in a list of plant materials to be grown in Charlemagne's garden (812 A.D.).

For more than two thousand years, the people of Japan, Korea and China have been eating the bulbs of *L. lancifolium* (until recently listed as *L. tigrinum*). This species was introduced to Europe in 1684 by Engelbert Kaempfer. Other lilies also serve as staples of Oriental diet.

Unlike most other bulbous plants, the bulbs of lilies have no protective tunic. Rather they consist of numerous overlapping scales, jointed together at the base. In this they resemble the genus *Fritillaria,* to which they are very closely related. Moreover, unlike other bulbs, the Lily bulb is not a device for storing food after a short growing season, but rather is an organ that enables the plant to winter over. Lily bulbs are therefore less self-sufficient than many others, and profit from higher nutrient levels in the soil than do most.

Few genera have undergone the tremendous changes that have occured in lilies within the last generation or so. The gardener before World War II was limited to species, many of them extremely beautiful, but many also difficult to grow and subject to diseases which rendered them short-lived in the garden. Today the picture has greatly changed, for it is largely hybrids, with improved disease resistance, that are available to the gardening public. These lily hybrids have larger and more brightly colored flowers in a wider range of color and type choices than the original species and are easier to grow. Furthermore, the species, imported from Holland or Japan, spent weeks in transit, packed in peat, or like some of those from Japan packed in night soil (not a pleasant material to handle!). Lily bulbs never totally go dormant; they must retain their live roots, and bulbs that have travelled great distances over a considerable period of time tend to lose them and perform poorly as a result.

90

L. longiflorum   *L. formosanum*

The first known lily hybrid was *L. x testaceum,* a natural cross between *L. candidum* and *L. chalcedonicum.* It is a trumpet lily with apricot-yellow flowers, and requires much the same treatment as *L. candidum* (see text). Gradually, interest arose in hybridizing lilies, and much interesting work was done in England, New Zealand, the United States and particularly in Canada. But the best was yet to come. In the early Thirties, Jan de Graaff, scion of a famous old firm in the Netherlands which specialized in Tulip and Daffodil production, founded Oregon Bulb Farms in Gresham, Oregon. He was fascinated by Lilies and collected species and their variants from all over the world. He then embarked on a breeding program that was to become one of the most successful ever undertaken in the world of horticulture, one which was entirely to change the face of the lily world. Building on work that had gone before and also on his own extensive knowledge and flair, he produced a stream of marvelous hybrids which were offered to the trade as clones or strains. Bigger flowers, new and better colors, increased disease resistance and ease of culture were the characteristics of his developments, which grew to dominate the modern world of lilies. Today, Oregon Bulb Farms is responsible for probably 75% of the world's lily production, and the species of yesterday have all but disappeared from the trade. In fact, in order to obtain many of the species, it is necessary to grow them from seed.

Lilium species and hybrids   LILY   Imbricate Bulb
Liliaceae: North Temperate Zones, Worldwide   Zone 3

USES: Garden, Cutting, Rock Garden (smaller types)

HABIT: Plants varying from 6 inches to 8 feet or more in height, blooming variously from mid-spring to early fall, in a wide range of colors, excepting blue. In addition to the 80 or more species, their natural variants and natural crosses, modern lily breeding has greatly enlarged the choice that gardeners have in this wonderful genus.

Lilies can be divided on the basis of their flower types into Trumpet-shaped, Turk's-Cap or Reflexed, Chalice-formed and Saucer-shaped types.

Some of the more important species include:

L. amabile. Korea. 18-36 inches tall, with narrow leaves marked with brown spots. Turk's-Cap, orange-red flowers with black spots in June and July. Tolerates full sun and dry soils. A parent of Jan de Graaff's Fiesta and Mid-Century Hybrids.

L. auratum. (Gold Band Lily) Japan. 3-8 foot plants with dark green, rather short and broad leaves. Large outward facing, Saucer-shaped flowers, white with spots and golden central band. Blooms in August and September. Best in moderate maritime climates, in light, often volcanic, acid soils. Shallow planting recommended. Many natural color variations. Highly fragrant. Bulbs are a source of food in Japan.

L. nepalense   L. philadelphicum

L. Brownii. Central China. 3-4 foot plants bearing Trumpet-shaped flowers, cream white with chocolate on the reverse.

L. bulbiferum. Europe. Plants to 4 feet in height, bearing bulbils in the upper leaf axils. Chalice-shaped orange flowers with red tips, sometimes flowers vary to yellow-orange.

L. canadense. Eastern North America. Plants 2-5 feet in height producing long rhizomes with bulbs at the ends. Whorled leaves. Pendent, Turk's-Cap flowers, yellow with black-purple spots are borne in June and July. Many color variations. Prefers damp, acid, well-drained soil.

L. candidum. (Madonna Lily). Cultivated in ancient Egypt, its place of origin is unknown. White, Trumpet-shaped flowers appear in June and July on 2½-6 foot plants. Not a stem-rooter, it makes a basal rosette of fall foliar growth, requires shallow (1-2 inch covering) planting and prefers a sunny situation and a calcareous soil. Plant late in summer or early in fall.

L. cernuum. Korea, Siberia and Manchuria. 1-3 foot plants with grass-like foliage. Fragrant lilac-pink Turk's-Cap flowers. A white form is also known. Grow in sun or light shade, sandy soil.

L. chalcedonicum. Greece. 2-4½ foot plants with lanceolate foliage and Turk's-Cap flowers, mandarin red with no markings, borne in July and August. Prefers a calcareous loam; very subject to botrytis.

L. Davidii. Western China. Widely cultivated in China as an edible. Plants to 5 feet bearing Turk's-Cap flowers, vermillion to scarlet and spotted black. There are many natural variations, including *Willmottiae* and *Maxwill,* once offered widely in the trade. A parent of Preston and Skinner hybrids.

L. formosanum. Taiwan. Plants to 6½ feet with grassy foliage and nodding white Trumpet-shaped flowers. Blooms late September and October, but in its native habitat, throughout the year. Short-lived and subject to virus.

L. Hansonii. Korea, Japan and Siberia. 2-5 foot plants with fragrant, Turk's-Cap nodding flowers, orange-yellow spotted brown. Blooms in June. Enjoys a natural immunity to virus. Easily grown in a soil rich in leaf mold and quite damp. Used by Jan de Graaff as a parent for his Paisley Hybrids.

L. Henryi. Central China. 5-8 foot plants with broad leaves. The Turk's-Cap flowers, orange with brown spots, are borne in July and August. A yellow form, spotted brown, is known. Virtually indestructible, it prefers a soil high in lime content.

L. japonicum. Japan. 3 foot plants with sparse, lanceolate leaves. Trumpet-shaped flowers, pink or white from May to August. Widely grown as an edible. Difficult to grow, subject to fusarium. Needs cool soil, well-drained, preferably near running water. Quite widely used in hybridization.

L. pumilum   *L. monadelphum*

L. lancifolium. *(L. tigrinum).* (Tiger Lily). China, Japan, Korea. 3-6 foot plants that produce axillary bulbils. Recurving orange-red flowers, strongly marked with chocolate brown. Blooms August-September. An important food crop in the Orient, where it is eaten as a starchy vegetable. Widely used in crosses.

L. longiflorum. (Easter Lily) Ryukyu Islands. 1-3 foot plants with white, Trumpet-shaped flowers in August and September. In nature, it grows in humus pockets in coral. Short-lived in the garden, best used as a pot or forcing subject. Various clones available.

L. Martagon. (Turk's-Cap Lily). Europe and Western Asia. 2-6 foot plants with hairy buds, opening to pendulous Turk's-Cap flowers, pink to carmine, usually spotted with brown. Variable as to color; white and purple forms are known. Best grown in well-drained, calcareous soils in light shade. Bulbs may remain dormant for a year after planting.

L. monadelphum. Northern Caucasus. 2-2½ foot plants, blooming in June with pendulous, Trumpet-shaped yellow flowers, flushed with pale lilac. Highly fragrant. Best grown in well-drained, humusy soils.

L. nepalense. Nepal. 4 foot plants with broad leaves and long, underground stems. Reflexed flowers appearing in July, green with purple on the inside. Of very limited hardiness.

L. pardalinum. (Panther Lily). California. 4-6 foot plants with orange-red Turk's-Cap flowers, mottled red-brown. July blooming. Grow in full sun, protected from the wind, in a moist, acid soil.

L. pensylvanicum (dauricum). (Candlestick Lily). Northeastern Asia. Chalice-shaped orange to red blooms in umbels atop 1-2½ foot plants. Prefers rich, damp, acid soils. Widely used in breeding, a parent of the Stenographer and Fighter Hybrids of Preston, as well as the Mid-Century Hybrids of Jan de Graaff.

L. philadelphicum. (Wood Lily). Central and Western North America. 1½-3 foot plants with Saucer-shaped flowers, bright orange-scarlet, shading to orange in the center and speckled in brown. There are many natural color variants. Grow, protected from rain and snow, in a free-draining loam, enriched with humus.

L. philippinense. Luzon. To 3 feet in height. White, Trumpet-shaped flowers in July and August. Of limited hardiness, good for cutting or pots.

L. pumilum (tenuifolium). (Coral Lily). Korea, through China and Manchuria to Siberia. 18 inch plants with grass-like foliage. Nodding, Turk's-Cap flowers, red, occasionally spotted with black, appear in June. Excellent in the rock garden or for cutting. Short-lived.

L. regale. China. Discovered at great personal peril by the famous E. H. Wilson at the turn of the century. 2½-6 feet with linear leaves. June blooming, with flaring, Trumpet-shaped flowers, white with a yellow throat and pink-purple on the reverse. Highly fragrant. Very easily grown in full sun in a soil high in humus. Protect with winter mulch. Long-lived.

93

L. regale   L. speciosum

L. rubellum. Japan. 1-1½ foot plants. Trumpet-shaped flowers in May, opening pale pink, then deepening to pink-purple. Fragrant. Demanding in its culture, *L. rubellum* requires very acid soil, much water and snow cover. Best planted in sphagnum-filled pots and grown in sun.

L. Sargentiae. Szechwan. 4-5 foot plants with dark green, broadly lanceolate foliage. Fragrant trumpet-shaped flowers, white with yellow in the throat, sometimes shaded pink, purple, green or brown on the reverse, open in July. Another E. H. Wilson discovery. Grow in a well-drained, rich soil where it will receive ample summer warmth.

L. speciosum. Southern Japan. 3-4 foot plants. Nodding, reflexed blooms, pink with white margins in August and September. White and red forms are known. Grow in full sun, with shade at the base, sheltered from the wind, and in a rich soil. Widely used to cross with *L. auratum* and *L. Henryi.*

L. superbum. Eastern North America. Plants varying from 4-8 feet with long stolons bearing bulbs at the end. Turk's-Cap flowers orange yellow with red tips and speckled throat in July and August. Many natural variations. Grow in sun, with shade at the base, in a well-drained, yet moist, acid soil.·

The modern hybrid lilies can properly be classified by the geographical origin of the species used to produce them or by the type of flowers in their genetic makeup. Thus:

Asiatic: Crosses using *L. bulbiferum, L. pensylvaticum, L. philadelphicum, L. pumilum, L. amabile, L. lancifolium, L. cernuum* and others.
    e.g. The Rainbow, Fiesta, Mid-Century, Golden Chalice and Harlequin Hybrids of Jan de Graaff; the Fighter and Stenographer Hybrids of Preston.

Turk's-Cap: Crosses using *L. Martagon, L. Hansonii* and others.   e.g. Painted Lady
    e.g. Painted Lady Hybrids of Kline, Paisley Hybrids of Jan de Graaff.

American: Crosses using *L. canadense, L. philadelphicum, L. pardalinum* and many others.
    e.g. Bellingham Hybrids.

Trumpet Hybrids: Crosses using *L. regale, L. Sargentiae, L. Brownii,* and although not a trumpet lily, *L. Henryi.*
    e.g. Such de Graaff originations as Olympic, Sunburst and Aurelian Hybrids, Heart's Desire, Yellow Regal and Green Mountain Strain.

Oriental: Crosses made from *L. auratum, L. speciosum, L. japonicum, L. rubellum.*
    e.g. Empress and Imperial series.

L. superbum

L. imperial Pink

L. Harlequin Hybrids

L. Oriental Hybrids

CULTURE: In the garden, almost without exception, lilies require excellent drainage. Plant in fall or early spring. (Because many types of lilies mature their bulbs late, they tend to be available in the trade later than other fall-planted bulbs. It is often helpful to select the site where your bulbs are to be planted, dig the hole and mulch heavily to prevent the soil from freezing. Then, when the bulbs arrive, they may be planted without difficulty.) Set bulbs 5-10 inches deep. (3 times their vertical diameter), depending on the size of the bulb. This deep planting is necessary, since most lilies produce two sets of roots, one set from the basal plate of the bulb and one from the stem above the bulb. Exceptions are *L. candidum* and *L. x testaceum,* which have no stem roots but produce a basal rosette of top growth in the fall. These should be planted in late summer and covered with only 1 inch of soil. *L. auratum,* another exception, although it is a stem rooter, it is so critical as to its drainage that planting about 3-5 inches deep is recommended. Most lilies prefer a location where they will receive full sun at their tops but shade at the roots so that the soil will remain cool. A mulch or ground cover will produce excellent results. While lilies are excellent for cutting, removing too much of the top growth will seriously reduce productivity the following year. To force, plant bulbs in a porous, well-drained medium, covering the bulbs with at least 2 inches of medium. Water thoroughly, then expose to at least 5 weeks of 33-38° F. temperature (or use bulbs previously precooled at those temperatures). After the cooling period, start at 50° F., then move to a sunny location at 60° F. night temperature after growth starts. *L. longiflorum* is particularly good for forcing.

Lycoris squamigera

Maianthemum

Lycoris species   MAGIC or RESURRECTION LILY   Bulb
                                      SPIDER LILY
Amaryllidaceae, China, Burma and Japan   Zones 3-8

USES: Gardens *(L. squamigera),* Pots, *(L. radiata group)*

HABIT: *L. squamigera* produces fragrant pink, trumpet-shaped flowers in August. They appear after the leaves, which sprouted in spring, have grown, died, and disappeared. Blooms are borne in umbels. The *L. radiata group* includes *L. radiata,* with reflexed flowers in rose, red or white on 1½ foot stems, June-August; *L. africana,* with golden yellow reflexed blossoms; *L. Caldwellii,* with pale yellow to white flowers; *L. Haywardii,* with red or purple blooms; *L. incarnata,* fragrant pink to rose-pink. Some are important as a florist's cut-flower crop.

CULTURE: Plant *L. squamigera* in late summer, 5 inches deep and 6-8 inches apart. Choose a location in full sun or light shade with good drainage. It performs best if left undisturbed over the years. *L. radiata* and its allies should be planted 3-4 inches deep. Above Zone 8, plant in spring and lift and store at 60° F. over winter.

The *L. radiata* group may also be grown most successfully in pots; in fact, this is their most important application. Use a regular potting mixture, to which has been added 1/3 coarse sand. Set bulbs with tips just at the surface, water and place in a sunny location with a night temperature of 60° F. Withhold further water until flower stalk appears, then keep moist until a month after blossoms fade. Then reduce water and feed every 2 weeks with soluble fertilizer. After the foliage dies down, keep dry until a new flower stalk appears and the cycle renews itself.

Maianthemum canadense   CANADA MAYFLOWER   Rhizome
                                   WILD LILY-OF-THE-VALLEY
Liliaceae, Canada and adjacent U. S. A.   Zone 3

USES: Ground Cover, Naturalizing in Shade

HABIT: A profuse, mat-forming plant with glossy 4-inch oval leaves and 6-8 inch racemes of white, fragrant flowers in May. Light red berries late summer and fall.

CULTURE: Easily grown in a shaded location in moist, acid, highly organic soils.

Maranta

Mertensia

Maranta species   PRAYER PLANT,   Rhizome, Tuber
                  ARROWROOT
Marantaceae, Tropical America

USES: Pots

HABIT: Clump-forming plants with broad, elliptical or lanceolate leaves, often with attractive colored markings. *M. bicolor* has elliptical green leaves marked with brown spots, and purple undersides; its flowers are white, marked with purple. *N. arundinacea* (Arrowroot) has lanceolate green foliage, somewhat similar to that of bamboo, and white flowers. A form with foliage variegated dark and light green with yellow is known.

CULTURE: Grow in pots containing a standard potting medium, keeping evenly moist and providing filtered light. A warm night temperature, such as that provided in most homes (65-70° F.), is ideal.

NOTE: *M. arundinacea* is the source of West Indian Arrowroot, a starchy substance used in cooking as a thickener for sauces and gravies.

Mertensia virginica   VIRGINIA BLUEBELLS   Tuberous Root
Boraginaceae, Eastern and Central U. S. A.   Zone 4

USES: Garden, Naturalizing

HABIT: Nodding bell-shaped flowers, pink in bud and opening to blue, borne in late April and May in clusters on 2 foot plants. The ovate, blue-green leaves die back to the ground by the end of June.

CULTURE: Plant in spring or (better) fall, in sun or partial shade. An acid soil, high in organic content is best, and plants will perform in direct proportion to the amount of moisture they receive. Leave undisturbed for 4-5 years before dividing and replanting.

Milla

Mirabilis

Milla biflora　　　MEXICAN-STAR　　　　　　　　　　　Corm
Amaryllidaceae, Southwestern U. S. A. to Central America　　Zone 8

USES: Garden, Rock Garden, Pots

HABIT: Grassy plants, bearing 12-18 inch flower stalks topped by 1-6 fragrant, 2½ inch white flowers, each with a green central stripe on each petal. Flowers are produced intermittently from spring to fall.

CULTURE: In the garden, where hardy (Zones 8 and south), plant in the fall, 3-4 inches deep and the same distance apart. Choose a sunny, well-drained situation.

In Zones 7 and above, grow as pot plants. Set in a well-drained mixture to which ground limestone has been added, 6 bulbs to a 5 inch pot, covering the bulbs about 1½ inches. Grow in a sunny window at a night temperature of 60° F. Keep moist and apply a soluble plant food monthly. After foliage dies back, withhold fertilizer and water until starting the next growing cycle.

Mirabilis Jalapa　　　FOUR O'CLOCK,　　　　Tuberous Root
　　　　　　　　　　　MARVEL OF PERU
Nyctaginaceae, Tropical America　　　　　　　　　　Zone 10

USES: Garden

HABIT: Bushy 3 foot plants with tubular fragrant flowers that open in the afternoon. Flower colors include reds, pinks, yellows and white, plus those with bicolor markings. A dwarf type is also offered in the trade. Plants flower for a long period in summer.

CULTURE: Usually grown as an annual, it is one of the easiest of all plants to grow from seed. It is, in fact, a tender perennial, and produces tuberous roots that may be lifted prior to frost and stored in peat at 55° F. over winter, to replant the following year. Plants take sun or partial shade in any garden soil.

Muscari   Muscari plumosa

Muscari species   GRAPE or PLUME HYACINTH   Bulb
Liliaceae, Mediterranean Region and Southwest Asia   Zone 3

USES: Garden, Naturalizing, Rock Garden

HABIT: Spring flowering plants with basal leaves and racemes of bell-shaped flowers, usually constricted at the mouth, in shades of blue or olive, or less often white, yellow or pink. Most are highly fragrant. *M. armeniacum* has deep purple flowers in autumn, grows to 9 inches, and its linear leaves appear in fall. *M. botryoides* usually has blue, but sometimes soft pink or white flowers, and bears its leaves in spring. *M. comosum,* (Tassel or Plume Hyacinth), grows to 18 inches, with strap-shaped leaves and long violet-blue inflorescences with the flowers shredded into tassels or plumes. *M. racemosum,* (Musk or Starch Hyacinth) is an exceptionally fragrant but also extremely aggressive species with broad leaves and purplish green flowers that fade to yellow.

CULTURE: Plant in fall, 3 inches deep and the same distance apart. Soil should be well-drained with no fertilizer added, since performance is best under conditions of low fertility. Full sun produces the best results. *Muscari* spreads rapidly, both from bulb offsets and from seeds, establishing large colonies in just a few years.

Narcissus

Div I - Unsurpassable   *Div II - Duke of Windsor*

The genus *Narcissus* is among the most important of all in our gardens, lending itself to a wide variety of uses and conditions—easily grown and familiar to all. The nodding yellow or white flowers are emblematic of spring and suggest to us the peace and serenity of a bucolic life which now, unfortunately, seems largely a matter of memory or hearsay.

At this point, let us clarify for you the classification of *Narcissus*. As with almost every popular flower, names are numerous and often confused. The terms "Daffodil", "Narcissus" and "Jonquil" have all been variously applied to this popular spring-blooming genus. Which then is right? "Narcissus", popularly applied to white and often cluster-flowered types, is the correct scientific or botanical name of the entire genus. "Daffodil", sometimes restricted to the large, usually yellow trumpet types, has long been applied in England, and is increasingly in the United States, as the popular or common name for the entire genus. "Jonquil" popularly (mis-) applied to the common yellow forms, is properly used for a species, *N. Jonquilla,* which has long, narrow rush-like leaves and multiple small yellow flowers with small cups.

The genus is widespread in nature, growing wild in Europe and North Africa, with great concentrations of species in the Iberian Peninsula and the Pyrenees. Narcissi were used in Roman times to heal wounds (we would very much discourage this use, since *Narcissus* has somewhat toxic properties, likely to cause dermatitis), and were very likely imported into England for that purpose by Roman soldiers.

Although widely grown in gardens in their wild form, as species or as their natural hybrids, Narcissi, unlike Tulips and other popular bulbous genera, were not popular subjects for the plant breeder's art until the middle of the Nineteenth Century. Further, unlike the other genera, the most important work was not done in Holland, (which we think of as synonymous with bulbs), but rather in the British Isles. The origin of modern Narcissi is primarily due to the breeding efforts of Edward Leeds, Manchester stockbroker, and of William Backhouse, Wolsingham banker, who were influenced to some extent by the early cross-breeder, the Rev. William Herbert of Manchester. Numerous members of the Backhouse family were active in this work, and it is to a Mrs. Backhouse that we owe the first important pink, which bears her name, and such mainstay varieties as Dick Wellband, Lady Diana Manners and the double, Texas. Important later work was done by Peter Barr, the famous plantsman and collector of Glasgow, by the Rev. George H. Engleheart of Salisbury, breeder of the famous white trumpet Narcissus, Beersheba, and by two Cornishmen, J. C. and P. D. Williams. To the credit of the latter go such standouts in today's gardens as Cragford, Carlton, St. Agnes, Scarlet Gem, Treviathan and Trousseau. Subsequent important contributions were made by A. M. Watson of Lincolnshire, an area in England with an important bulb industry, and by Dr. N. Y. Liver. Across the Irish Sea, three great breeders developed more multiple-award winners than all the rest in *Narcissus* breeding history. The Brodie of Brodie whose numerous standouts include Coverack Perfection, Hunter's Moon, Whitely Gem, and that most beautiful of all white trumpets, China Clay. Guy L. Wilson (1887-1962), of Ulster, gave us, among many others Broughshane, Cantatrive, Chinese White and Moonstruck. J. L. Richardson (1890-1960) introduced such gems as Bahram, Galway, Green Island, Krakatoa, Limerick, Music Hall and

Div V - Thalia   *Div VI - February Gold*

Salmon Trout. Nor were the Holland breeders without accomplishment. G. Lubbe of Oegsgeest developed Actaea and Yellow Sun, while from Degraaf Bros. of Noordwijk came Ada Finch, Daisy Schaeffer, Gertie Miller and Golden Perfection. Most recently, the Leenen Family of Sassenheim has contributed many lovely varieties. In the United States, Oregon Bulb Farms, famous for its lilies, bred many fine Narcissi, too, while in Canby, Oregon, Grant Mitsch can rightly be called "The Giant of American Narcissus Breeding".

Although breeding of Narcissi is relatively modern, the genus has been grown and collected with enthusiasm for hundreds of years. The first treatise on Narcissi in English dates back to the middle of the Sixteenth Century, and British writers on garden subjects have been discussing Narcissi with enthusiasm and in detail ever since. But it was the various species, not the hybrids, that were so widely grown; in fact, the species were grown to an extent far greater than they are today.

Narcissus species & hybrids   DAFFODIL   Bulb
Amaryllidaceae, Europe and North Africa   Zone 3

USES: Garden, Naturalizing, Rock Garden, Pots

HABIT: 3-20 inch plants with fragrant flowers in white or yellow or combinations thereof, blooming for the most part in early spring, although a few species, little grown today, bloom in fall. As they endure for many years in the garden, there have been thousands of varieties developed and registered, of which hundreds are still offered in the trade.

In the interest of bringing some order out of chaos, the Royal Horticultural Society, the registering body for new *Narcissus* introductions, has formulated the following classification system for the genus. The illustrative examples are ours, using, wherever possible, varieties available in the trade:

DIV I—Trumpet (corona) as long or longer than perianth segments. 1 flower to stem.
  a) Perianth colored, corona colored, not paler than perianth. e.g. King Alfred, Unsurpassable.
  b) Perianth white, corona colored. e.g. Trousseau, Music Hall.
  c) Perianth white, corona white, not paler than perianth. e.g. Mt. Hood, Beersheba.
  d) Any color combination not described above. e.g. Spellbinder.

DIV II—Large-Cupped Narcissi. 1 flower to stem, cup or corona more than 1/3 but less than equal to the length of the perianth.
  a) Perianth colored, corona colored, not paler than perianth. e.g. Hyperion, Kissproof.
  b) Perianth white, corona colored. e.g. Duke of Windsor, Chinook.
  c) Perianth white, corona white, not paler than perianth. e.g. April Snow, Gypsy Moth.
  d) Any color combination not described above. e.g. Binkie, Gleeful.

102

Div VII - Suzy   *Div IX - Actaea*

DIV III—Small-Cupped Narcissi. 1 flower to stem, cup or corona not more than 1/3 the length of the perianth.
  a) Perianth colored, corona colored, not paler than perianth. e.g. Alcida, Irish Coffee.
  b) Perianth white, corona colored. e.g. Aircastle, Lady Kesteven.
  c) Perianth white, corona white, not paler than perianth. e.g. April Clouds, Tern.
  d) Any color combination not described above. e.g. Reversa.

DIV IV—Double Narcissi. e.g. Cheerfulness, Golden Ducat.

DIV V—Triandrus Narcissi
  a) Cup or corona not less than 2/3 the length of the perianth segments. e.g. Liberty Bells, Thalia.
  b) Cup or corona less than 2/3 the length of the perianth segments. e.g. April Tears, Hawera.

DIV VI—Cyclamineus Narcissi
  a) Cup or corona not less than 2/3 the length of the perianth segments. e.g. February Gold, Tete-a-Tete.
  b) Cup or corona less than 2/3 the length of the perianth segments. e.g. Little Imp, Lofty.

DIV VII—Jonquilla Narcissi
  a) Cup or corona not less than 2/3 the length of the perianth segments. e.g. Desert Song, Golden Guinea.
  b) Cup or corona less than 2/3 the length of the perianth segments. e.g. Finch, Suzy.

DIV VIII—Tazetta Narcissi. e.g. Cragford, Geranium.

DIV IX—Poeticus Narcissi. e.g. Actaea, Andrew Marvel.

DIV X—Species, Wild Forms and Wild Hybrids.
These are the Narcissi that alone graced gardens throughout the world until the beginning of *Narcissus* breeding about 1850. They include species, natural variations within species, and natural hybrids. With the advent of the thousands of man-made cultivars, many of their precursors have disappeared from the trade, which seems rather a shame. Included here are just a few:

N. Pseudonarcissus. Native to Europe. Plants with leaves to 15 inches and solitary yellow flowers whose trumpet or corona exceeds in length the perianth segments. This is probably the major parent of the DIV I Narcissi of today.

N. minor. Sometimes referred to as *N. minimus,* this is a tiny little fellow growing to 6 inches with nodding solitary flowers, each of which has a soft yellow perianth and deep yellow corona just shorter than the perianth segments. From Europe.

N. Jonquilla. Rush-like leaves to 18 inches. Clustered, highly fragrant yellow flowers with the corona less than half the length of the perianth segments. There is a double form. Southern Europe and Algeria.

Div X - Jonquila Simplex

Div X - N. Bulbocodium conspicuus

N. Bulbococium. (Hoop and Petticoat N.) Rush-like leaves to 15 inches, perianth segments very narrow and streamer-like. The one-inch corona resembles the hoop-skirts of a bygone era. Bright yellow. The variety *citrinus* is lemon yellow, while var. *conspicuus* has larger flowers. Southern France and the Iberian Peninsula.

N. cyclamineus. A native of Spain and Portugal with 12 inch narrow leaves and solitary, drooping flowers with sharply reflexed perianth and wavy-edged corona as long as the perianth segments. Deep yellow.

N. poeticus. The fragrant Pheasant's-Eye *Narcissus*, whose flowers are used to a considerable extent in the perfume industry. Growing to 18 inches, with solitary flowers with white perianth and very short corona, yellow or green with a wavy red edge. Var. *recurvus* has recurved segments. France to Greece. Prefers early planting and a rather heavy soil.

N. Tazetta. (Polyanthus N.) The Paperwhite Narcissus. To 18 inches with clustered fragrant flowers. Typically it is white in both its perianth and cup, but white forms with yellow cups (Chinese Sacred Lily) or yellow with deeper yellow cups (N. Soleil d'or) are also known. Possibly these are natural hybrids. These Narcissi are familiar to all as the bulbs you forced as a child in the house in pebbles and water. Native to the Mediterranean Region, they may be of somewhat more limited hardiness than others.

N. triandrus. (Angel's Tears). 1 foot plants with rush-like leaves and typically pure white flowers, with the cup about half the length of the perianth segments. White and yellow or all-yellow forms are known. Native to the Iberian Peninsula.

N. juncifolius. 6 inch plants with rush-like foliage and bright yellow flowers with darker coronas borne 1-4 to the stem. The corona is half the length of the perianth segments. From Southern France and Spain.

N. serotinus. A fall-blooming species, native from Spain to the Near East and growing about 10 inches tall with linear leaves. The flowers, 1-2 to the stem, are white with a white or greenish corona (sometimes orange), less than half the length of the perianth segments.

N. viridiflorus. This is a rare bird indeed, for not only does it bloom in the fall, but the flowers are green! Borne 2-4 to the 1½ foot stem, the nodding blossoms have 1 inch perianth segments that are reflexed and spidery. Native to Morocco, it prefers a rather moist location and is of limited hardiness.

N. x odorus. A natural hybrid between *N. Pseudonarcissus* and *N. Jonquilla,* this is the well-known Campernelle. It has narrow 1 foot leaves and bright yellow fragrant flowers up to 2½ inches across, the corona at least half the length of the perianth segments. A double form is available. From Southern Europe.

Lobularis

Gold Collar

N. x gracilis. Another natural hybrid, this time between *N. Jonquilla* and *N. poeticus,* with grassy 1 foot leaves and lemon yellow flowers, often with darker corona. From Southern France.

DIV. XI—Split-Corona Narcissi. Corona split for at least 1/3 of its length. e.g. Lemon Beauty, Cassata.

DIV. XII—Miscellaneous Narcissi. All Narcissi not falling into any of the above Divisions. e.g. Donna Bella, Elfhorn.

CULTURE: In the garden: plant bulbs in early fall (early planting permits roots to establish before winter), setting large-flowered types 5-6 inches deep and 6-8 inches apart and smaller bulbs 3 inches deep and 4-6 inches apart. Choose a well-drained location in sun or light shade. Some of the species, particularly those of Iberian derivation, prefer a rather dry, poor soil. In any event, little fertilizer is needed. After flowering, allow foliage to ripen and die back completely before cutting. Divide when excessive foliage and few flowers indicate bulbs are too crowded.

Naturalizing: Naturalizing is the practice of making plantings with little apparent plan so that the material looks as if it grew there naturally. Narcissi are a favorite subject for such treatment. Actually, some considerable planning is necessary to achieve the desired result. To begin with, while mixtures "for naturalizing" are widespread and offered at low prices, better and more natural looking results are obtained by planting groups of a single variety or species in irregular groups. These may be informally planted along wooded or meadow walks, or in areas which are visible from a window or other frequented portion of your property. Spacing of bulbs should be further apart than in the garden, so that division will not be necessary. Space the groups in an irregular fashion, with some running one into the other and some fairly widely apart. Remember that various varieties bloom at different times and those planted in partial shade bloom later than those in warm, sunny locations. In this way, a longer period of bloom can be provided. Narcissi are virtually free of troubles, and naturalized plantings will last almost forever, increasing in numbers and providing a spring picture of unrivaled beauty.

Forcing: Bulbs of some DIV IX varieties, and of the Paper-White kinds in DIV X can be grown easily in water, using pebbles, children's marbles, or vermiculite for support, and will bloom in 6 to 8 weeks from starting. Start in a cool, preferably dark place until roots form, then bring into the light. Many Narcissi in the other divisions may be forced in pots in the following manner: Using a standard, well-drained potting medium, pot several bulbs in a 5 or 6 inch pot, covering the tips with about ½ inch of medium. Early-blooming varieties do best, water thoroughly. Place pots in a cold frame where they will receive about 6 weeks of near-freezing temperature. After this precooling, bring indoors and grow at 50° F. night temperature, watering generously after growth appears.

Neomarica

Nerine

Neomarica gracilis   TWELVE-APOSTLES,   Rhizome
WALKING IRIS
Iridaceae, Tropical Americas   Zone 10

USES: Pot Plant, Hanging Baskets

HABIT: Plant with sword-shaped 2-2½ foot leaves, often of semi-reclining habit. Iris-like flowers, white with yellow, brown and blue markings are produced in the same fashion as *Iris,* and are then followed by small plantlets, which, weighing down the flower stalks, touch the soil and take root. Thus the name "Walking Iris".

CULTURE: One of the easiest plants to grow, requiring no particular soil or care, just ample light.

NOTE: This was one of the favorite house plants of grandmother's (or perhaps great-grandmother's) day. Not widely known or grown today, this splendid plant deserves a resurgence of popularity.

Nerine species   Bulb
Amaryllidaceae, South Africa   Zone 9

USES: Pots, Cutting, Garden

HABIT: Plants have green or blue-green foliage, and bear long-lasting clusters of reflexed, lily-like flowers in white and shades of pink or red. *N. curvifolia* has curving, deciduous foliage that develops after the scarlet flowers; *N. falcata,* white flowers tipped pink and twisted foliage that is produced at the same time; *N. flexuosa,* pink or white blooms; *N. sarniensis* (this name is often erroneously applied to *Lycoris radiata),* red, rose or pink flowers and rather wide leaves developing after flowers.

CULTURE: Plant in regular potting medium, so that half the bulb is above the surface of the medium. Water thoroughly and grow in a brightly lit situation at a night temperature of 55° F. After the initial watering, grow on the dry side until the flower stalk appears, then keep moist through flowering and as long as the foliage continues to grow. When foliage stops growing, withhold water to induce dormancy, allow bulb to rest, and begin cycle once again.

Ophiopogon   *Orchis*

Ophiopogon japonicus   DWARF LILYTURF,   Tuberous Root
                                  MONDO GRASS
Liliaceae, Japan, Korea   Zone 6

USES: Ground Cover, Edging, Pot Plant

HABIT: Dark green leaves, resembling grass but much thicker, and grow-ing to form a dense turf 8-10 inches high. 6-part flowers, light lilac in color, borne in small nodding clusters and followed by pea-sized fruits of soft, iridescent blue.

CULTURE: Best planted in spring, 6 to 8 inches apart in sun or shade. Widely tolerant of different soils, but performs best with ample year-round moisture. Also occasionally grown as pot plant under normal household conditions.

Orchis species   Rhizome, Tuberous Root
Orchidaceae, North America and Eurasia

USES: Wild Garden

HABIT: Spring and summer blooming plants with flowers of white, pink, rose or red-violet. Leaves are basal, often large and glossy. Blooms are frequently pleasantly fragrant.

CULTURE: Grow under conditions of constant moisture, in a soil enriched with humus or leaf mold, in a situation where they will recieve good air circulation and good drainage. Mulch to conserve moisture.

Ornithogalum umbellatum   *Ornithogalum thyrsoides*

Ornithogalum species   STAR OF BETHLEHEM   Bulb
Liliaceae, Mediterranean Europe, North Africa and Western Asia

USES: Border, Pots, Cutting, and Dried Arrangements

HABIT: Winter and spring blooming bulbous plants 2-36 inches tall usually bearing erect stalks of star-shaped white, yellow or orange-red flowers. Many are fragrant. *O. arabicum* is white with a black pistil. *O. caudatum,* (Pregnant Onion) has white flowers marked with green, but is grown more as a curiosity for its pendant, strap-shaped leaves and for its strange habit of producing bulblets under the skin of the exposed mother bulb. *O. miniatum* includes white, yellow and orange forms, *O. thyrsoides* (Chincherinchee) bears white flowers in dense racemes that last exceptionally well when cut. *O. umbellatum* has white flowers.

CULTURE: *O. umbellatum* is hardy to Zone 4 and should be planted in fall in sun or light shade in a rich, sandy, well-drained soil. Under such conditions it will colonize and multiply rapidly. Set bulbs 2-3 inches deep and 6-8 inches apart, keep amply moist during the growing season and topdress with a balanced fertilizer or an application of well-decomposed compost.

O. arabicum, O. miniatum and *O. thyrsoides* are tender bulbs and are grown indoors in pots. Start in fall or winter in a light, well-drained potting mixture, 1 bulb to a 5 inch pot, barely cover with the medium, grow in a sunny location, and maintain a night temperature of 50° F. Water moderately as growth begins, freely during active growth until flowers fade, and withhold water to induce dormancy. While foliage is growing, use soluble fertilizer, applied at ½ the recommended strength, every 2 weeks. *O. caudatum* is grown in much the same manner, except that the bulb is planted so that only the basal plate is in the soil and the remainder is above the surface.

Oxalis species   WOOD SORREL   Bulb, Tuber, Rhizome
Oxalidaceae, World-wide   Various

USES: Garden, Rock Garden, Pots (tender species)

HABIT: There are over 800 species of *Oxalis,* distributed world-wide, with particularly heavy concentrations in South America and South Africa. They are low-growing plants, with clover-like foliage which often closes up at night, as do the flowers. Flowers, in a wide range of colors, are borne singly or in umbels. Among the hardy species are: *O. adenophylla,* from South America, whose 6 inch plants bear bright pink or sometimes rose-purple flowers in early summer. *O. violacea,* a North American native, grows to 10 inches and has purple flowers.

Oxalis

Pachyrhizus

Among the numerous tender species are *O. Acetosella,* from Asia, often offered in the trade as the Shamrock of Hibernian fame. Its white flowers, occasionally veined in rose or purple, appear in early spring. *O. Bowiei,* often a weed under greenhouse benches, has a creeping habit and small yellow flowers; *O. Deppei,* sold as the Good-Luck Plant, has four-part leaves and red or sometimes white flowers and grows to over 1 foot in height.

CULTURE: In the garden, plant in full sun 2 inches deep and 3 inches apart. Soil should be well-drained; a fairly sandy one is best. The plants rest in spring.

In pots, using a sandy or gritty potting medium, plant in early fall, setting just below the surface, 6 to a 6-inch pot. Water thoroughly, then set in a cool place, out of direct sun, and keep on the dry side until growth starts. Then bring to full light, increase watering and fertilize with liquid plant food or a slow-release fertilizer. After flowering, gradually reduce water until foliage matures, then store in pots under cool conditions until early Autumn; then divide and replant.

Pachyrhizus species	YAM BEAN,	Tuberous Root
	JICAMA	
Leguminosae, Mexico, Central and South America		Zone 10

USES: Food Crop

HABIT: Vining perennial plants with rhomboidal or oval leaves and clustered fragrant flowers, much resembling purple or white sweet peas. They often grow to 15 or 20 feet in height and are cultivated for their tubers which resemble water chestnuts in texture and flavor. Both *P. erosus,* from Mexico and Central America, and *P. tuberosus,* from the Amazon Region, are grown. Seeds of both are toxic.

CULTURE: Pachyrhizus may be grown from seed or from the tuberous roots. Since the plants require a long, warm growing season to mature their tubers, starting from small tubers, when available is likely to result in more and larger roots. Grow in full sun in a light, deeply cultivated soil, rich in potash, planting about 6 inches deep in rows 2-3 feet apart, with about 12 inches between plants in the row. Keep well watered until established, then apply a heavy summer mulch and keep the vines pinched back to about 5 feet. For best production, remove flowers as they form. Harvest just prior to frost (vines will have started to die) clean them without washing, and store cool.

Paeonia

Panax

Paeonia species and cultivars   PEONY   Rhizome
Paeoniaceae, China, Tibet and Siberia   Zones 3-8

USES: Garden, Cutting

HABIT: Discussed here are the herbaceous peonies which grow from a 'rhizome. Tree Peonies (*P. suffruticosa* derivatives), are not included. Most herbaceous garden Peonies are cultivars of *P. lactiflora.* They grow to 5 feet in height with attractive, often lobed foliage and large single, semi-double or double, fragrant flowers in May and June. Hundreds of cultivars in many different forms are known and available in the trade. They have inspired so much interest that they have become a hobbyist's flower, with many fine plant breeders devoting their lives to the improvement of the plant. Garden peonies are among the hardiest and longest-lived of plants, with individual specimens known to have grown and flowered for over 100 years. The Fern-Leaved Peony, *P. tenuifolia,* grows 1½-2 feet in height with finely divided, fern-like foliage, and flowers in pink, rose or red. A double form is known.

CULTURE: Plant in early fall, selecting a sunny location and a well-drained, slightly acid soil. In the southernmost portion of their range, partial shade may produce better results, as heat is detrimental to their performance. Enrich soil with humus or compost. Plant 3 feet apart, covering the "eyes" or growing tips of the rhizomes with no more than 1 inch of soil. Deeper planting will likely lead to "blindness"; that is, failure to flower. Peonies are heavy feeders, so fertilize each spring and fall, using 5-10-5 and avoiding the use of manure which could encourage fungus problems. Allow foliage to grow until it dies back in late summer, then remove and burn, to avoid spread of fungal disease.

Panax quinquefolius   AMERICAN GINSENG   Rhizome
Araliaceae, Eastern and Central U. S. A.   Zone 3

USES: Naturalizes in moist, shaded woodlands. Grown primarily for its roots which have alleged medicinal properties.

HABIT: Plants 1-2 feet tall with greenish-white leaves usually in whorls of 5 and 5-petaled flowers in June followed by bright red ½-inch fruits.

CULTURE: Plant rhizome 2 inches deep in deeply worked, highly organic soil in a shaded location. *Panax* will not tolerate full sun. Drainage should be good, but soil should be constantly moist. Cover bud to a depth of 2 inches, being careful not to injure it in planting. Do not fertilize or cultivate. While Ginseng grows best in the shade of trees in the forest, this may not be practical for commercial production and lathe shade may be substituted. Harvesting is best done in late fall or winter after dormancy occurs; two to three years from planting is required to harvest a crop.

X Pardancanda

x Paschia

X Pardancanda Norrisii
Iridaceae

Rhizome
Zone 6

USES: Garden

HABIT: A bigeneric hybrid between *Belamcanda* and *Pardanthopsis*, having Iris-like foliage and flowers varying in form from Iris-like to flaring. The color range is extremely wide, including solid colors and many blooms with attractive markings. Blooms from July to frost on plants to 4 feet in height.

CULTURE: Easily grown in almost any soil, except under conditions of standing water. Highly drought resistant, it performs best in full sun. Plant 1-2 inches deep and about 6 inches apart, in either fall or spring.

X Paschia
Gesneriaceae

Tuber

USES: Pots

HABIT: A gesneriad of unknown parentage, but undoubtedly descended in part from *Sinningia*. Foliage is quite similar in form to the familiar florist's "Gloxinia". Flowers, which face sideways, are frilled and bright scarlet or red purple.

CULTURE: Set the tuber concave side up, in a peaty medium, covering with no more than 1 inch of the medium and using a 6 inch pot for each tuber. Place in filtered light or grow under artificial lights, at a night temperature of no less than 65° F., keeping moist at all times while in growth. Plants will benefit from high humidity, so misting, or a tray of pebbles over which water is poured, is recommended. After a period of active flowering, plants will die back and go dormant, during which time water should be reduced to a bare minimum. When growth starts again, increase water. Feed with soluble fertilizer, applied every 2-3 weeks during the growing season.

Pecteilis

Peltiphyllum

Pecteilis radiata   HERON OR EGRET FLOWER   Tuber
Orchidaceae, Japan

USES: Pots

HABIT: Erect leafy stems to 2 feet in height topped with single or clustered 1 inch flowers with soft green sepals and white petals, beautifully fringed and spurred.

CULTURE: Plant 3 tubers to a 5 inch pot; barely cover the growing tip with a rich, loose, well-drained potting mixture. Water thoroughly and place in a sunny window; keep amply moist until after flowering. The plants will then enter a period of dormancy and should be in cool, dry storage for 3-4 months, after which the cycle can be started anew.

Peltiphyllum peltatum   UMBRELLA PLANT   Rhizome
Saxifragaceae, Pacific Northwest   Zone 5

USES: Shaded Borders, Naturalizing, Waterside Plantings

HABIT: In early to mid spring, 12 inch, leafless flowering spikes spring unheralded from the ground, each bearing terminal clusters of rich pink flowers. These are followed by 10 inch peltate leaves, each on a 4 to 5 foot stalk. The result is an almost unbelievably lush, tropical effect.

CULTURE: Easily grown in a cool, moist soil in shade or partial shade. Adapts marvelously to waterside plantings.

Physalis

Pleione

Physalis species   CHINESE LANTERN,   Rhizome
                       HUSK or GROUND CHERRY
Solanaceae, The Americas and Japan   Various

USES: Dried Arrangements, Food Crop

HABIT: Relatives of the Tomato, growing 2-4 feet in height, with alternate leaves and bladder-like flowers, usually yellow. The fruits, which are round berries, are enclosed in a papery husk. *P. Alkekengi,* often offered as *P. Franchetti,* has large showy husks that turn bright orange in fall and are often grown to cut, dry and use in winter arrangements. *P. ixocarpa* (Tomatillo), with yellow or purple fruit, is grown in Mexico as a food crop. *P. peruviana* (Cape Gooseberry), has small yellow fruit often made into preserves. *P. pruinosa* (Husk or Strawberry Tomato), has small edible yellow fruit and often is grown in the vegetable garden.

CULTURE: Grow in a warm, sunny situation, in any average garden soil that is provided with good moisture. *Physalis* require a long growing season to produce the best fruits and to attain the desired color in the case of the ornamental species. *P. pruinosa* is generally grown from seed, much as a tomato. Provide winter mulch in Northern areas.

NOTE: *P. Alkekengi* is an extremely aggressive plant. Care should be taken to plant it in an area with mechanical restraint to its spreading, or you will be up to your ears in Chinese Lanterns!

Pleione species   Cormlike
Orchidaceae, East Asia

USES: Garden, Pots

HABIT: Spring blooming terrestrial orchids 8 inches tall, with broad plicate leaves and attractive, heavily fringed flowers in shades of pink or purple with various markings.

CULTURE: In the garden, plant in a cool, shady location barely covering the "corm" with soil, which should be very well-drained and high in humus. In cooler areas, a heavy winter mulch is recommended.

Plant individual pseudobulbs in a pot no larger than 4 inches in diameter. Fill pots with an osmunda and peat mixture, and provide extra drainage materials such as pot shards or gravel in the bottom. Keep moist during the growing season and provide full sun during winter months, filtered light during the summer. A night temperature of 60° F. or below is ideal. Plants enter dormancy from October through February, during which time water should be withheld and pots stored cool. Feed during active growth with an organic fertilizer such as liquid fish emulsion.

113

Podophyllum

Polemonium

Podophyllum peltatum   MAYAPPLE, WILD JALAP   Rhizome
Berberidaceae, Eastern and Central North America   Zone 3

USES: Shaded Wild Garden

HABIT: Large, lush green, palmately lobed leaves resembling umbrellas opening, pop up from creeping underground roots. Nodding white flowers appear in early spring, followed by yellow fall fruit. A somewhat aggressive grower that rapidly colonizes the area in which it is planted, providing cover of cool, rich beauty.

CULTURE: Plant 1-2 inches deep and 15-18 inches apart preferably in moist woodsy soil, high in humus and partially shaded. If ample moisture is provided, it will tolerate sunnier situations.

NOTE: Supposedly, the fruit are edible and can be made into delicious preserves. We would rather hesitate to do so, since the bitter resin, podophylin, is derived from the stems and roots. Somewhat toxic, it is used in pharmacology as a cathartic.

Polemonium species   JACOB'S LADDER   Rhizome
Polemoniaceae, North and South America, Europe and Asia   Zone 2

USES: Border, Naturalizing, Combining With Spring Bulbs

HABIT: Pinnately compound leaves resembling the rungs of a ladder give this plant its common name. *P. caeruleum* has blue flowers in April and May on plants from 1-3 feet in height, depending on the variety. *P. reptans* has blue flowers in late spring and early summer on 2 foot plants. A white form also exists.

CULTURE: Widely tolerant of growing conditions, but performs best in a rich, highly organic soil. Will stand full sun in the northern part of its range, prefers partial shade further south. Leaves tend to wilt in extremely hot weather.

Polianthes   *Polygonatum*

Polianthes tuberosa   TUBEROSE   Rhizome
Agavaceae, Mexico   Zone 7

USES: Garden, Cutting

HABIT: Late summer blooming plants, 15-42 inches tall, bearing highly fragrant white flowers in terminal clusters. Both single and double flowering forms are available in the trade.

CULTURE: Tuberoses require a long growing season. Plant in spring after danger of frost is past, in a sunny location with good, well-drained sandy garden soil enriched with organic matter. Set 2 inches deep and about 6 inches apart. Staggered plantings will yield a succession of bloom. Supply ample water during active growth and fertilize monthly with a balanced garden fertilizer. It is best, even in zones where they are winter hardy, to lift the bulbs in the fall, allow them to dry for a few days, remove dead foliage and store in a cool location over winter.

NOTE: Widely grown as a cut flower and used in southern France as an ingredient of perfume.

Polygonatum commutatum   SOLOMON'S SEAL   Rhizome
Liliaceae, North America and Mexico   Zone 4

USES: Shaded Border, Naturalizing

HABIT: Graceful arching stems with oval leaves and white bell-shaped flowers borne in loose clusters in May and June. Blue berries in fall. A variegated form with green edged white leaves, and growing 2-2½ feet in height, is available.

CULTURE: Grow in shade or partial shade in a deep, rich organic soil with ample moisture and a low pH.

Puschkinia

Ranunculus

Puschkinia scilloides   STRIPED SQUILL   Bulb
Liliaceae, Asia Minor and The Caucasus   Zones 3-9

USES: Garden, Rock Garden, Border

HABIT: Spring flower, 4-8 inch plants bearing clustered blue and white striped flowers. The narrow foliage dies back in early summer.

CULTURE: Plant in fall in sun or partial shade. A well-drained, sandy loam, enriched with organic matter is best. Set bulbs 2-3 inches deep and about the same distance apart. Keep watered in spring after growth appears and fertilize with 5-10-5. Leave bulbs undisturbed for several years.

Ranunculus asiaticus   PERSIAN BUTTERCUP   Tuberous Root
Ranunculaceae: Southeastern Europe and Southeastern Asia   Zone 8

USES: Garden, Cutting, Pots

HABIT: 12 to 18 inch plants with flowers resembling double buttercups and measuring up to 4 inches across, borne in late spring and summer, depending upon where grown. Colors include white, shades of yellow, orange, pink and red. Foliage is graceful and fern-like.

CULTURE: In Zones 8-10 plant in late fall for winter and early spring bloom; elsewhere, plant in spring. Before planting, soak tubers for several hours in water. The tuberous roots, which resemble small, petrified bunches of bananas, should be set 4 inches deep, so that the crowns remain somewhat dry while the roots are moist. Water at planting time, then not again until growth is evident. Dig in fall and store in dry peat or vermiculite at 55° F.

For pot culture, soak rootstocks and set in a sandy, extra well-drained mixture at a depth of 1½ inches. Water after planting, then place in a sunny situtation with a night temperature of 50-55° F. Keep on the dry side until growth appears, then increase watering as long as plants are growing actively. Let tubers dry off and rest for 2-4 months, then resume cycle.

Rheum   *Rhodohypoxis*

Rheum species   RHUBARB   Rhizome
Polygonaceae, Asia   Zone 3

USES: Edible, Borders (rarely)

HABIT: Plants with bold leaves in basal clumps and racemes of small flowers, white or red during early summer. *R. officinale,* a native of Western China, was introduced into Europe by Marco Polo. It is used as an ornamental, and its rhizome is also used for medicinal purposes. *R. Rhabarbarum,* usually incorrectly listed as *R. Rhaponticum,* (the leaves of this plant are poisonous, only the leaf stalk is used as a food) is the common rhubarb of pie fame, and comes from Manchuria.

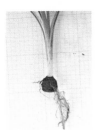

Rhodohypoxis Baurii   Rhizome
Hypoxidaceae, South Africa   Zone 8

USES: Rock Garden, Border Foreground

HABIT: Tiny (3 inch) plants with narrow leaves and six-segmented flowers in rose or white, also in white streaked with rose.

CULTURE: Grow in full sun in a well-drained, sandy soil. Near the northern limits of its hardiness, a winter mulch is beneficial.

Rodgersia

Rodgersia species   Rhizome
Saxifragaceae, China, Japan and Korea   Zone 5

USES: Garden, Waterside Plantings

HABIT: A genus, closely allied to *Astilbe,* with bold, exceptionally attractive broad foliage, often lobed, and spikes of white, cream or pink flowers in summer. *R. aesculifolia* grows to 6 feet, with broad, crinkled leaves, often bronze-tinted, and has cream or pink blossoms. *R. pinnata* has pinnately arranged leaves and cream flowers marked with pink. A white form is known. *R. podophylla* has large, palmately compound leaves, grows to 5 feet and has rather inconspicuous cream blooms. *R. sambucifolia* attains a height of 3 feet, with pinnate leaves and handsome sprays of white flowers. *R. tabularis* has huge, rounded, somewhat lobed peltate leaves of light green and contrasting, cream-white flowers.

CULTURE: Easily grown in sun or partial shade, *Rodgersia* require a moist soil and do well even on the edge of a marsh. These are large, bold plants and should be set about 2 feet apart.

Sanquinaria

Sansevieria

Sanguinaria canadensis   BLOODROOT   Rhizome

Papaveraceae, Eastern North America   Zone 3

USES: Partially Shaded Garden, Naturalizing

HABIT: Large white starry flowers with yellow anthers above silvery green lobed leaves on 8 inch plants. Flowers with an unusually satiny texture appear in April. Plants go dormant in summer and fall. Single, semi-double and double forms are available. The red color of the stems, roots and sap give rise to the common name.

CULTURE: Easily grown in sun or partial shade in a highly organic soil with ample moisture. Ideal conditions are full sun during the spring and partial shade during the summer. Water during periods of drought. Profits from a summer mulch.

Sansevieria species   SNAKE PLANT,   Rhizome
                            BOW-STRING HEMP
                            MOTHER-IN-LAW-TONGUE
Agavaceae, Tropical and South Africa   Zone 10

USES: Garden (where hardy), Pots

HABIT: Stiff, upright plants with succulent leaves, often barred or margined in contrasting colors. The fragrant, usually white flowers appear, at irregular intervals, in long, rather loose racemes. The most commonly grown are: *S. trifasciata,* with sword-shaped leaves to 4 feet, variously marked or margined. A dwarf variety is commonly cultivated. *S. Ehrenbergii* has bluish leaves arranged in a fan; *S. zeylanica* forms a spreading rosette of leaves to about 2 feet.

CULTURE: One of the most easily grown and long-lasting of house plants, resisting practically every abuse from almost total neglect to occasional applications of cigarette ash and the dregs of martinis. It was one of the most widely grown of house plants in Grandmother's day, primarily for its cast-iron disposition. It withstands poor light and low humidity. For best results, and to produce the flowers that Grandmother rarely saw, it should, however, be grown with moderate moisture in a sunny location.

Sarracenia

Sarracenia species   PITCHER PLANT   Rhizome
Sarraceniaceae, Eastern North America   Zones Various to 3

USES: Bog Garden, Terrarium

HABIT: One of the more important members of the group of carnivorous plants, with basal, hollow, fluted leaves, forming trumpets topped by a lid. The leaves hold water and act as fly traps: the plants exude a sweet substance near the top of the leaves; this attracts flies and other insects which are then unable to escape because of the downward-pointing hairs on the inside of the leaves; they fall into the water and are digested and absorbed by the plant. Flowers are showy, with bright, short-lived petals and persistant sepals. The hardiest of the genus, *S. purpurea,* has greenish brown leaves suffused with purple, and purple flowers; it grows wild as far north as Labrador. *S. flava* has yellow flowers up to 4 inches across and yellow-green leaves, with crimson throat (leaves are sometimes entirely red), and grows as tall as 4 feet. *S. rubra* has maroon flowers and green leaves striped with purple.

CULTURE: Outdoors, Sarracenias require a highly acid medium—a mixture of sphagnum and sand produces the best results—and a constant supply of water, along with high humidity. Bog or swamp gardens can provide these conditions, the conventional border cannot.

Indoors, they are best grown in a terrarium or pot tented over with a plastic bag. Use a sand base, then a thick layer of moist, unmilled sphagnum moss, covering rhizomes to the depth of about one inch. If a pot is used, stand it in a dish of water to help keep it constantly moist; an enclosed terrarium will achieve this on its own. Grow in filtered light and a fairly cool (55-60° F.), night temperature. Try to avoid watering with hard water.

Scilla

Scilla natalensis

Scilla species   Bulb
Liliaceae, North Africa, Southern Europe and Asia Minor   Various

USES: Garden, Naturalizing, Mass Planting, Rock Garden (hardy species), Pots (tender species)

HABIT: The hardy species are mostly spring blooming (one, *S. autumnalis,* is an exception) and grow to about 6 inches in height. *S. bifolia* has a pair of linear leaves and produces a loose raceme of nodding ½ inch flowers, typically in blue, but also occasionally in white or rose-pink. *S. siberica* has ribbon-shaped leaves and deep blue ½ inch flowers. Various shades of blue and a white form are known. *S. Tubergeniana* has larger flowers, to 1½ inches, predominantly white, tinged and striped with blue. Of the tender species, *S. natalensis,* from South Africa, grows to 3 feet and bears a stout raceme containing 50-100 blue flowers; *S. peruviana* (a misnomer, since it comes from the Mediterranean region) has strap-shaped leaves, grows to 1½ feet and also produces stout racemes of bluish flowers on long pedicels. *S. campanulata* (hispanica) is properly *Endymion hispanicus,* and is discussed there, while *S. socialis* is properly classified under *Ledebouria socialis.*

CULTURE: The hardy species are planted in sun or partial shade, 2-3 inches deep and 5-6 inches apart. Choose a well-drained location, but one where the plants will receive ample moisture during the active growing season in spring. Given this, they will colonize nicely. Foliage dies back in early summer. Scillas do best in cool areas. (Zones 3-8).

The tender species are potted in fall in a standard potting medium, just covering the top of the bulb, and grown at 55-60° night temperature. Water sparingly until growth starts; then increase watering during active growth, until flowers are spent. After flowering decrease water, allow foliage to ripen and die back, then store in pots at 50° until time to restart the cycle.

121

Sinningia   *Sinningia cardinalis*

Sinningia speciosa   GLOXINIA   Tuber
Gesneriaceae, Central and South America

USES: Pots

HABIT: Compact plants to 1 foot in height with 4-6 inch hairy leaves and velvety trumpet or slipper-shaped flowers in red, purple, violet, pink and white, either solid colors or with white edges or occasionally blotches and spots. Double forms are available in the trade. They are among the best of "bulbous" plants for the house, producing many flowers over a long blooming period, and, for the most part, well adapted to normal household conditions.

CULTURE: Set the tuber concave side up, in a peaty medium, covering with no more than 1 inch of the medium and using a 6 inch pot for each tuber. Place in filtered light or grow under artifical lights, at a night temperature of no less than 65° F., keeping moist at all times while in growth. Plants will benefit from high humidity, so misting, or a tray of pebbles over which water is poured, is recommended. After a period of active flowering, plants will die back and go dormant, during which time they should be watered only very occasionaly, enough to keep the soil from becoming completely dry. When growth starts again, increase water. Feed with soluble fertilizer, applied every 2-3 weeks during the growing season.

Sinningia cardinalis   CARDINAL FLOWER   Tuber
Gesneriaceae, Brazil

USES: Pots

HABIT: Compact plants with several pairs of hairy ovate leaves, bright green often variegated with darker green, and 2 inch flowers of brilliant scarlet.

CULTURE: Grow as for *Sinningia speciosa.* High humidity will markedly extend the blooming period.

Smilacina　　　　　　　　　　　　Smithiantha

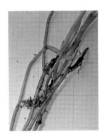

Smilacina species　　　FALSE SOLOMON'S-SEAL　　　Rhizome
Liliaceae, North America　　　　　　　　　　　　　　　　　Zone 4

USES: Wild Garden

HABIT: Plants from 1 to 3 feet in height with alternate ovate or lanceolate leaves with prominent veining. Flowers are white, pink or purplish and appear in late spring followed by red, sometimes spotted fruit. *S. racemosa* grows 2-3 feet in height, *S. sessilifolia* is somewhat shorter, and *S. trifolia* is a dwarf grower that requires highly acid, boggy soils and very cool conditions.

CULTURE: Grow in an acid, highly organic soil in full to partial shade. (Partial shade will do well in the northern portion of their range; elsewhere full shade produces best results). Requires ample moisture; keep watered during dry summers to retain the good appearance of the attractive foliage.

Smithiantha　　　TEMPLE BELLS　　　　　　　　　　　　Rhizome
Gesneriaceae, Mexico

USES: Pots

HABIT: Long known as *Naegelia*, these are splendid pot plants, both for their attractive, velvety foliage and for their spikes of brightly colored, nodding, bell-shaped flowers. *S. cinnabarina* has red stems, leaves that are red-purple above and green marked with purple on the reverse, and brilliant flowers, scarlet on the outside and cream with red spots inside. It grows to about 2 feet. *S. multiflora* has green leaves and cream white flowers. *S. zebrina* has dark green hairy leaves variegated in purple, and scarlet red flowers marked with yellow and orange. There are many hybrids in the trade, embracing a wide range of colors.

CULTURE: Plant rhizomes about 1 inch deep in a rich, moisture-retentive medium, high in peat content. Grow in a warm, sunny situation (or under lights), keep constantly moist and provide extra humidity by setting the pots on trays of pebbles over which water has been poured. After flowering has ceased (usually early winter), dry off and store warm for 3 months, then start up again.

Solanum tuberosum

Solanum tuberosum   WHITE or IRISH POTATO   Tuber
Solanaceae, Peruvian Andes

USES: One of the world's most important food crops.

HABIT: Plants with pinnate leaves and flowers white or bluish. Stems are rather weak and grow to about 3 feet in length. Grown for their edible, starchy tubers, many cultivars are in commerce, varying in color of skin, tuber size, maturity date, suitability for various cooking methods and disease resistance.

CULTURE: Divide tuber into several pieces, each containing one or more eyes, and cure for a week or more under conditions of high humidity at a temperature of 60 to 65° F. Several weeks before date of last frost plant 2 to 3 inches deep and 12 to 15 inches apart in the row, with 2½-3 feet between rows. Potatoes have extremely high nutrient requirements so soil should be heavily fertilized at the time of planting, with additional side-dressing fertilizer applications during the growing season. A soil pH of 5.4 or below is required to prevent scab disease. Potatoes require cool growing conditions to produce tubers; in southern areas they are often grown as a fall or winter crop. Ample moisture is also required; in dry areas, irrigation is necessary. As plants grow, gradually mound up soil around them until the rows are elevated about 6 inches. "New" potatoes may be harvested as ready, potatoes for storage should be dug after vines mature and die back from frost. Wash or brush off dirt and store in a dark place at 50° F. or below.

NOTE: The potato has an amazingly interesting history and has played a major role in the economy and population distribution of the world. Cultivated by the Incas in the Peruvian Andes, it was first recorded by a Spanish explorer, Juan Castellano. Introduced to Spain, it was grown and then in turn exported as a food crop to the Spanish colonies. The relief of the ill-fated Jamestown colony also brought to England the potato, which allegedly was introduced to Ireland by Sir Walter Raleigh (who has been blamed for all sorts of things). The potato rapidly became the major item of the Irish diet—so much so that when the crop failed in three successive years, 1845-47, tens of thousands starved and many more emigrated, thus popularizing the vegetable in North America. So, to a crop failure we owe a substantial portion of our population, our most important vegetable crop, and the folk song: "The Praties They Grow Small".

Sparaxis   *Spathicarpa*

Sparaxis species   HARLEQUIN or WANDFLOWER   Corm
Iridaceae, South Africa   Zone 9

USES: Garden, Rock Garden, Cutting, Pots

HABIT: Spring blooming plants 18-24 inches tall with sword-shaped,
gladiolus-like foliage and 12-18 inch spikes of 2-inch flowers in red, yellow,
blue, purple or white, often with brightly contrasting throat markings. In
addition to various hybrids, the species *S. grandiflora,* yellow or purple,
and *S. tricolor,* in various combination of white, yellow, purple or brown,
are commonly grown. Others, often referred to as "Sparaxis", are properly
of the genus *Dierama.*

CULTURE: In those parts of Zones 9 and 10 that experience dry, rainless summers, plant in
fall in a sunny, well-drained soil, 2-3 inches deep and 4-6 inches apart. Elsewhere, they are best
grown in pots, started in the fall. Plant 6 to a 5 inch pot with the tops 1 inch below the surface of
the well-drained potting mixture. Set in a cold frame and mulch with 4 inches of peat or straw.
When shoots are 1 inch tall, expose to light in the cold frame until the shoots turn green, then
transfer to a 50° F. night-temperature greenhouse. Water moderately until growth is vigorous,
then increase watering until flowering ceases. After flowering is over, ripen corms by gradually
withholding water and exposing to full sun. Keep dry until fall, when the cycle can be repeated.

Spathicarpa sagittifolia   FRUIT SHEATH PLANT   Rhizome
Araceae, South America

USES: Pots

HABIT: Attractive pot plant about 1 foot tall with membranous leaves
shaped like arrowheads, and a recurved green spathe to which is united the
spadix bearing separate male and female flowers in rows along the middle.

CULTURE: Easily grown in a standard potting medium kept uniformly
moist. Conventional household temperatures suit it well, as does filtered light or partial shade.

125

Spathiphyllum

Sprekelia

Spathiphyllum species and hybrids Rhizome
WHITE ANTHURIUM
Araceae, Pantropics

USES: Pots. Outstanding plant for low-light conditions, frequently employed in decorating commercial buildings.

HABIT: Long, glossy green leaves, long-lasting white flower spathes with white spadices. Occasionally fragrant. Attractive for foliage effect even when not in bloom. Plants offered are sold as *S. Clevelandii* or *S. Mauna Loa;* both are hybrids of unknown derivation, perhaps from *S. floribundum.*

CULTURE: Among the easiest to grow and most satisfactory of house plants, they require little light and minimal attention. Grow in soil or potting medium high in organic content, keeping moist at all times. Does well at normal household temperatures of 65-75° F.; best grown under conditions of low light intensity. *Spathiphyllum* will survive and grow even in a room away from the window, but requires slightly more light (filtered), to flower.

Sprekelia formosissima AZTEC or JACOBEAN LILY Bulb
Amaryllidaceae, Mexico Zone 8

USES: Pots

HABIT: 12-18 inch strap-like leaves surround blooming spikes bearing several crimson flowers, 3 inches across with rather narrow, ribbon-like flower parts.

CULTURE: Pot in spring in a highly organic mixture, with the neck of the bulb above the surface of the medium. Water sparingly until growth starts, growing at a night temperature of 60-65° F. Keep moist during active growth and feed monthly with soluble plant food. After growth dies back, store dry at 45° F.

Sternbergia

Streptanthera

Sternbergia lutea   LILY-OF-THE-FIELD   Bulb
Amaryllidaceae, Southeastern Europe and Southeastern Asia   Zone 6

USES: Garden, Rock Garden

HABIT: 2 inch yellow, crocus-like flowers borne in September on 4 inch stems. The 12 inch, strap-like leaves remain green throughout the winter and wither the following spring.

CULTURE: *Sternbergia* demands extremely good drainage. Failure to prosper and flower usually indicates excess moisture, but in areas where the drainage requirements are met, the bulbs will flourish and multiply, and may be left alone for years. Plant in summer, in full sun in a dry, extremely well-drained location. Set bulbs 5 inches deep and 3-4 inches apart. Apply a coarse winter mulch, such as salt hay or straw, in colder areas.

Streptanthera species   Corm
Iridaceae, South Africa

USES: Pots

HABIT: Low growing plants, less than a foot tall, with fan-shaped clusters of leaves and rather poppy-like flowers with a pronounced central eye. *S. cuprea* is bright orange or pink with a purple central zone marked with yellow spots; *S. elegans* is white or cream with yellow throat marked with purple. Both are late spring blooming.

CULTURE: Plant corms, 1 to a four-inch pot, in late fall and keep cool (50° night) until growth starts, watering only sparingly. When growth commences, move to a sunny location at a night temperature of 60-65° F., keeping evenly moist and occasionally applying a dilute soluble fertilizer. After flowering ceases, withhold water, allow foliage to die back, and start cycle again in early winter.

Symphytum   Synnotia

Symphytum species   COMFREY   Tuberous Root
Boraginaceae, Europe and Western Asia   Zone 4

USES: Border, occasionally grown as a potherb or for alleged medicinal values.

HABIT: Rather coarse herbaceous perennials with spring flowers in coarse scorpioid cymes. *S. caucasicum* grows to 3 feet, with showy pink buds that open to rich blue and very much resemble *Mertensia. S. x uplandicum* (Russian Comfrey) grows to 5-6 feet with flowers of red, purple, yellow, white or rose changing to purple.

CULTURE: Plant about 3 feet apart in virtually any soil as long as the plants will receive ample moisture. Plants will survive, but with limited vigor, in dry areas. Best left undisturbed once established.

NOTE: In folk medicine, comfrey was supposed to help in the healing of broken bones. We recommend an orthopedic surgeon!

Synnotia species   Corm
Iridaceae, South Africa   Zone 9

USES: Garden, Pots, Cutting

HABIT: Plants have linear or sword-shaped leaves, and grow to 1½ feet, with irregular, funnel-form flowers in purple or yellow, growing in loosely branched inflorescences. *S. Metelerkampiae* has linear foliage, grows to 1 foot, and has purple flowers; *S. villosa* grows to 1½ feet with yellow flowers marked with purple.

CULTURE: Prefers a light, well-drained soil, setting 4-6 inches deep and 6 inches apart. Fertilize with 5-10-5 at planting time, and again as flower spikes develop. Keep well-watered. To provide a succession of bloom, make staggered plantings at 2 week intervals, starting when danger of frost is past and continuing through mid-July. Staking is desirable. While *Synnotia* may winter over in southern areas, they are best dug when foliage yellows. Allow to dry in the sun, remove dead foliage, discard the old, spent corm and store the new ones dry at 40-50° F. over winter.

Tacca

Talinum

Tacca Chantrieri   BAT FLOWER   Rhizome
Taccaceae, Southeastern Asia

USES: Pots

HABIT: Plants 2-3 feet in height with corrugated foliage and 6 inch flowers of dusky maroon-black, resembling the wings of a bat, and adorned with a series of long "whiskers".

CULTURE: Plant 1 to a 6 inch pot, in a highly organic, moisture-retentive potting mixture. During active growth place in a warm, moist location under very subdued light. Feed every several weeks with an organic plant food. After flowering, usually in late summer or early fall, the plant will go dormant, and watering should be reduced until signs of new growth appear, when the cycle should be repeated.

Talinum paniculatum   JEWELS-OF-OPAR   Tuberous Root
Portulacaceae, Southern U. S. A. to Central America   Zone 9

USES: Garden, Containers

HABIT: 2 foot plants with elliptical leaves and panicles of red or yellow flowers in summer. A form with leaves edged in white is also grown.

CULTURE: In the garden, grow in a sunny situation and a fertile soil. Mulch in winter at the northern limit of hardiness.

In pots, use a standard potting mixture and grow in a sunny situation at a night temperature of 55-60° F. Fertilize with soluble plant food every few weeks during active growth.

Tecophilaea

Tigridia

Tecophilaea cyanocrocus   CHILEAN CROCUS   Corm
Tecophilaeaceae, Chilean Andes   Zone 8

USES: Garden (where hardy), Pots

HABIT: Early spring blooming plants, to 6 inches tall with blue, bell-shaped flowers marked with white in the throat and along the veins of the tepals.

CULTURE: In the garden, plant about 3 inches deep in a sunny location, where they will receive ample moisture during the spring blooming season and little during the rest of the year. A well-drained, sandy soil is best.

In pots, plant about 7 to a 6-inch pot, covering with about 1 inch of well-drained planting medium. Water and grow at 60° F. night temperature in a sunny situation. When growth starts, supply ample water until flowers are spent, then reduce moisture and water minimally the rest of the year.

Tigridia Pavonia   TIGER or SHELL FLOWER   Bulb
Iridaceae, Mexico, Central and South America   Zone 7

USES: Garden

HABIT: Gladiolus-like plants, 12-30 inches in height with brightly colored 3-6 inch flowers. Many named cultivars are available in the trade, including white and various shades of yellow, orange, pink and red, often with spotted and contrasting centers. The individual florets last only a day, but each stem bears several florets, and a bulb may produce several flowering stems during its blooming season in July or August.

CULTURE: Plant in spring after nights no longer drop below 55° F. Set in a sunny location, in a well-drained soil, 3-4 inches deep and 4-8 inches apart. Keep soil moist and top-dress with 5-10-5 several times in the course of the growing season. In Zone 7 and south, bulbs may be over-wintered in the ground, lifting and dividing every 3-4 years. North of Zone 7, dig bulbs after foliage yellows, dry, remove dead foliage and store in dry peat or perlite at 60° F. over winter.

NOTE: *Tigridia* bulbs have been eaten for centuries by the Indians of parts of Mexico. They are reported (we have no first-hand knowledge of this) to taste like chestnuts.

Tolmiea

Trillium

Tolmiea Menziesii   PIGGYBACK PLANT   Rhizome
Saxifragaceae, Western North America   Zone 5

USES: Ground Cover, Woodland Garden, Pots, Hanging Baskets

HABIT: Bright green cordate or ivy-shaped hairy leaves cover the mounded evergreen plants that may reach 12 inches in height. The summer-borne, brownish-purple flowers are of little landscape value. A natural curiosity, since new leaf buds arise from the old leaves at the junction of petiole and leaf, creating a tiered effect. These new leaves can be detached to propagate new plants.

CULTURE: Grow in partial shade in a moist, organic soil. Spreads rapidly. Indoors, it is a widely used house plant that will grow under conditions of moderate light. Keep evenly moist and grow at about 60° night temperature.

NOTE: In addition to its unusual growth habit, *Tolmiea* is remarkable in being one of the few hardy indigenous plants which is widely grown indoors as well.

Trillium species   WAKEROBIN   Tuberous Root
Liliacaea, North America, The Himalayas and Eastern Asia   Zone 3

USES: Shady Garden, Naturalize in Moist Woodland

HABIT: Low-growing, spring-blooming plants with their flower parts grouped in threes, subtended by a single whorl of three leaves. *T. erectum* grows to 2 feet, with flowers in white, red-purple, green or yellow, followed by dark red fruit. *T. grandiflorum,* perhaps the best-known and showiest, has white flowers in April and May, which mature to pink and are followed by blue-black berries. *T. sessile* has attractively mottled foliage and flowers brown-purple, dark red or yellow. *T. undulatum* has rather nodding flowers of white veined in purple and grows to 20 inches.

CULTURE: Grow in partial shade in rich, well-drained humusy soil. A constant supply of moisture is required, so water during periods of drought. Removing the single whorl of leaves is fatal to the plants. Most species prefer quite acid soils; *T. sessile* does best in soils that are neutral or only slightly acid.

Tulbaghia

Tulbaghia violacea   SOCIETY GARLIC   Corm
Liliaceae, Tropical and South Africa   Zone 9

USES: Garden (Zones 9-10), Pots

HABIT: Umbels of 1 inch pink or purple flowers borne atop leafless flower stalks from October to April in the garden and from March to November indoors. The evergreen leaves are 1 foot long. The corms, and sometimes other plant parts, have an onion-like odor, hence the common name.

CULTURE: Where hardy, set in the garden with the tips of the corms just even with the soil surface, planting 8-12 inches apart. A very well-drained sandy soil, enriched with organic matter, and a sunny location are preferable.

In pots, use a well-drained potting medium, keep moist and grow in a sunny location at a night temperature of 50° F. Feed monthly with a soluble plant food.

Tulipa

Rembrandt Tulips   *Darwin Tulips*

Legend has it that a Persian youth, in desperate pursuit of his ladyfriend, was thrown from his horse and killed. Wherever a drop of his blood fell, there arose a red Tulip. Touching as the story may be, it is undoubtedly apocryphal, but the actual story of the Tulip is a more fascinating one than today's TV dramas.

The earliest known illustration of a Tulip is on a vase found at the Palace of Minos at Knossos, in Crete, and dates back to 1600 B.C. Many wild species of Tulips are native to the Middle East, Central Europe, and the area which we now think of as the Cradle of Civilization. Exactly when they began to be grown as garden flowers we do not know; certainly they were widely grown long before they first appeared in literature in the work of Omar Khayyam, well before 1200 A.D., and later in the poetry of Hafiz (who referred to tulips as "Lale") in 1390.

In the 1500's, Augustus Geslenius Busbequis (Busbecq) was appointed Austrian Ambassador to the court of Suleiman The Magnificent, Sultan of Turkey. He found extensive plantings of Tulip flowers in the Royal gardens and elsewhere and reported on them. Through some language confusion, they were described as "Tulliband", (the Turkish word for "turban", from the Persian "Dulband"), although the flowers themselves were called "Lale".

The Tulips grown at court in Turkey were not the wild species, but rather highly sophisticated hybrids. The rules for judging of these hybrids were as stringent as those for a garden club floral arrangement; the standards were carefully set forth, and the ideal strongly resembled the Lily-Flowered Tulips of today.

Tulips were subsequently illustrated and described by Konrad von Gesner in 1560, and were sent by Busbecq to his friend, the great botanist Carolus Clusius (Charles de L'Ecluse), in Prague. It was he who was largely responsible for their spread in Europe, and more particularly for their introduction to Holland, for when he moved to Leyden, in Holland, to head the botanical gardens there, he brought his Tulips with him.

Tulips were first mentioned in English writing in Lyle's translation of Dodoeus (1578). They were referred to again in 1582 by Richard Hakluyt, who wrote requesting a friend who was traveling to Constantinople to bring back some bulbs for him.

Interest in Tulips became widespread, and much work was done to develop new varieties. Just as the Turks had their ideal of what a perfect Tulip should be, so too did the Dutch, and in the production of cultivars that approached this ideal, they had a six-legged ally. For the Dutch ideal was the "broken" Tulip, with fantastically swirled color patterns, resembling finger painting. The cause of the "breaking" was the virus-caused Mosaic disease, spread by aphids and other sucking insects. Incidentally, today's Rembrandt Tulips are the product of such breaking which becomes genetically fixed.

The interest in Tulips and Tulip breeding became even more widespread, and new varieties, or those considered to be outstanding, sold for increasingly large sums of money. Speculation in them started, particularly in Holland, but also elsewhere in the Continent and even in England. The equivalent of tens of thousands of dollars, either in money or sometimes in livestock and

Parrot Tulips

Double Late Tulips

even household possessions, was invested in one, sometimes as yet non-existent bulb. This speculation, or Tulipomania ("windtrade" to the Dutch) had many of the aspects of the commodity futures market of today, and has been compared by one critic to the rather heedless purchase of objects of art by today's cognoscenti. Then, on February 3, 1637, the bottom dropped out of the Tulip market, with a crash similar to that fateful October day in 1929. The Tulipomania was over, leaving behind many wrecked fortunes and lives.

But the interest in Tulips for their beauty and as a staple of commerce was in no way diminished, and the breeding and growing of them became an established industry in Holland. Considerable breeding work also was done in France, Belgium and England. And the growing of Tulips spread, too, with the first importation of bulbs into the New World in 1716. Today, they are almost commonplace throughout the range where they can be successfully grown, and are loved for their bright colors in the garden and for their excellence as cut flowers.

Tulipa species and hybrids TULIP	Bulb
Liliaceae, Central Asia and Asia Minor	Zones 3-8

USES: Garden, Rock Garden (dwarfer types), Cutting

HABIT: 3-30 inch plants, usually with blue-green, but occasionally with purple and brown-mottled foliage, and cup-shaped flowers in a complete range of colors excepting blue. Both single and double-flowered forms are found. Blooming period is from March through May, depending upon the type of cultivar or species.

The *Classified Register of the Royal General Bulb Growers of the Netherlands* divides Tulips into 15 classifications or divisions as follows: (In all cases, the examples are ours):

EARLY FLOWERING

DIV I—Single Early Tulips. e.g. Keizerskroon, White Hawk, General de Wet.

DIV II—Double Early Tulips. e.g. Murillo, Albrecht Durer, All Gold.

MID-SEASON FLOWERING

DIV III—Mendel Tulips. Chiefly the result of crosses between the old Duc van Tol and Darwin Tulips, generally not having the habit of Triumph Tulips. e.g. Ajax, Olga, Premier.

DIV IV—Triumph Tulips. Chiefly the result of crosses between Single Early and late (May Flowering) Tulips; plants of stouter habit than Mendel Tulips. e.g. Aleppo, Makassar, Korneforos.

T. Kaufmanniana T. Greigii

DIV V—Darwin Hybrid Tulips. Chiefly the result of crosses between Darwin Tulips with Tulipa Fosteriana and the result of crosses between other Tulips and botanical Tulips which have the same habit and in which the wild plant is not evident. e.g. General Eisenhower, Gudoshnik, Oxford.

LATE FLOWERING

DIV VI—Darwin Tulips. Lower portion of flower usually rectangular in outline; segments of good substance; stems tall and strong. e.g. Flying Dutchman, Dreamland.

DIV VII—Lily-Flowered Tulips. Flowers with pointed, reflexed petals. e.g. Golden Duchess, Marcellina, White Triumphator.

DIV VIII—Cottage (Single Late) Tulips. Flowers oval, which do not belong to Divs VI or VII. e.g. Mrs. J. T. Scheepers, Smiling Queen, Reine Victoria.

DIV IX—Rembrandt Tulips. Broken Tulips, striped or marked brown, bronze, black, red, pink or purple on red, white or yellow background. e.g. Dainty Maid, Goldfinder, Insulinde.

DIV X—Parrot Tulips. Tulips with laciniated flowers, generally late-flowering. e.g. Fantasy, Blue Parrot, Texas Flame.

DIV XI—Double Late (Peony Flowered) Tulips. e.g. Symphonia, Mount Tacoma, Angelique.

SPECIES. Wild plants and hybrids in which the wild plant is evident.

DIV XII—Kaufmanniana. Varieties and hybrids. Very early flowering, sometimes with mottled foliage. e.g. Cesar Franck, Shakespeare, Stresa.

DIV XIII—Fosteriana. Varieties and hybrids. Large, early flowering, some cultivars with mottled or striped foliage. e.g. Madame Lefeber (Red Emperor), Purissima, Princeps.

DIV XIV—Greigii. Varieties and hybrids. Always with mottled or striped foliage, flowering later than Kaufmanniana. e.g. Red Riding Hood, Dandy.

DIV XV—Other species and their varieties and hybrids.

These include (the listings and descriptions are ours, there are many others.)

T. australis. North Africa and the Iberian Peninsula. Yellow, tinged red or green. 8 inches tall.

T. Batalinii. Central Asia. Lemon yellow with brown base, 6 inches tall (this is possibly a yellow form of *T. linifolia*).

T. biflora. South Russia. White with yellow eye. Very small in all its parts, this tiny little fellow grows to just 5 inches.

T. Clusiana   T. Kolpakowskiana

T. Clusiana. (Peppermint-stick Tulip, Lady Tulip). Iran to Afghanistan. White with carmine-red reverse with white margin and violet base. 12 inches tall.

T. cretica. Crete. White, outside tinged purplish red. 8 inches tall.

T. dasystemon. Central Asia. Bright yellow. Outer segments violet. 7 inches tall.

T. Didieri. Southern Europe. Red, reverse tinged crimson, tips of tepals slightly reflexed. Base purple with cream margin. 12 inches tall.

T. Eichleri. Turkestan. Scarlet red, black base, usually with yellow margin. 8 inches tall.

T. galatica. Asia Minor. Pale yellow, marked with olive green on the reverse. Base olive green. Late blooming. 8 inches tall.

T. Hageri. Greece and Crete to Western Asia Minor. Dull red, reverse tinged with green. Black base with yellow margin. 12 inches tall.

T. ingens. Central Asia. Bright scarlet, black base. 10 inches tall.

T. Kolpakowskiana. (What a dirty trick to play on a pretty, inoffensive little bulb!) Central Asia. Yellow, reverse streaked with red. A variable species in nature. 6 inches tall.

T. kuschkensis. Central Asia. Scarlet with black base and yellow margin. Requires extreme heat and very dry soil. 9 inches tall.

T. lanata. Central Asia. Orange-scarlet with black base and yellow margin. 20 inches tall.

T. linifolia. Central Asia. Scarlet with black base. 6 inches tall.

T. Marjolettii. Southeastern France. Pale creamy white, edged cerise. Very late flowering. 24 inches tall.

T. oculus-solis. Southern Europe. Scarlet, tinged with green and brown on the reverse. Early. 8 inches tall.

T. praecox. Northern Italy to Turkey. Brick red, marked with yellow stripe, base olive black with yellow margin. Inner tepals shorter and narrower, giving triangular effect when in bud. 20 inches tall.

T. praestans. Central Asia. Multiflowered, having light scarlet blooms with yellow median stripe. Base olive black with yellow margin. Inner tepals shorter and narrower than outer ones. 12 inches tall.

T. primulina. North Africa. Cream white, tinged purplish brown on the reverse. Yellow base. Opens in the afternoon. Fragrant. 8 inches tall.

T. saxatilis. West Africa, Europe, Asia Minor. Yellow with greenish reverse. A multi-flowered species with small (to 2″ long), fragrant flowers. 12 inches tall.

T. turkestanica. Central Asia. White with gray-violet on reverse. Base orange-yellow. 8 inches tall. Multiflowered.

T. urumiensis. Iran. Yellow, marked olive and red on the reverse. 5 inches tall.

137

T. praestans

T. turkestanica

T. Uremiensis

T. linifolia

CULTURE: In the garden, plant in fall in a sunny, well-drained location, setting bulbs 6-8 inches deep and 5-6 inches apart. Planting depth will vary with the texture of the soil; deeper in light soils, more shallow in heavy. Also since garden Tulips (DIV I-XI) tend to "run out" in a year or two, partly as a result of the bulbs dividing, their life can be prolonged and division delayed by setting at a depth of 9-11 inches, provided drainage is adequate. Fertilize with balanced fertilizer when growth becomes evident in spring. Allow foliage to ripen and die back after flowering. The tulip species, particularly those with woolly tunic-linings, require a hot, dry location with little summer water and no fertilizer for best performance.

TO FORCE: Select early-blooming varieties and plant 5-6 bulbs to a 6 inch pot, covering the tips of the bulbs with ½ inch of well-drained potting medium. Water, then place pots in the cold frame where they will get 6 weeks of near-freezing temperature. Bring into a light situation and grow at 50° F. night temperature.

Uvularia

Vallota

Uvularia grandiflora   MERRYBELLS   Rhizome
Liliaceae, Eastern North America   Zone 3

USES: Naturalizing

HABIT: Vigorous 12-30 inch perennial with lemon yellow, pendulous flowers from April to June. Green, oval, perfoliate leaves.

CULTURE: Grow in a well-drained, highly organic soil of neutral or slightly acid reaction, in at least partial shade.

Vallota speciosa   SCARBOROUGH LILY   Bulb
Amaryllidaceae, South Africa   Zones 9-10

USES: Garden (Zones 9-10), Pots

HABIT: Clusters of scarlet red flowers, borne in late summer and early fall on 2 foot stems. Foliage is evergreen and strap-like, and measures up to 24 inches in length.

CULTURE: Where hardy, plant in the garden in early summer or after flowering in the fall. Partial shade and a well-drained sandy soil to which organic matter has been added is preferable. Set bulbs with tips barely covered and 15-18 inches apart, since the plants form luxuriant clumps of foliage.

Indoors, plant in pots, allowing no more than 1 inch between bulb and edge of pot, as *Vallota* does best when potbound. Keep moist during the growing season and feed every month with a soluble plant food, such as Hyponex. Grow at a night temperature of 55° F. in a sunny location. Reduce water when active growth is over. Add fresh soil when repotting.

Vancouveria

Veltheimia

Vancouveria species INSIDE-OUT-FLOWER Rhizome
Berberidaceae, Western North America Zone 5

USES: Ground Cover, Border

HABIT: Plants with small cordate or rounded leaflets, somewhat resembling those of *Aquilegia,* and purple or brown in some species. They grow 1-1½ feet in height and bear arching panicles of flowers in early summer. *V. chrysantha* has evergreen leaves and yellow flowers; *V. planipetala,* white or purple blooms, and *V. hexandra,* a deciduous species, white flowers.

CULTURE: Easily grown in any garden soil from the lightest sand to the heaviest clay, in light conditions ranging from full sun to full shade.

Veltheimia viridifolia CAPE LILY Bulb
Liliaceae, South Africa Zone 9

USES: Pots

HABIT: Plants with attractive basal leaves with wavy margins. In midwinter, a flower spike with clustered florets resembling *Kniphofia* (Red-Hot Poker), but in soft cream-yellow suffused pink, is produced. Even without the flower, the plant is among the most attractive and interesting of house bulbs, just for its foliage effect.

CULTURE: Select a pot that will allow for 1 inch of clearance between the bulb and the rim. Using a standard potting mixture, set the bulb so that the upper half is above the surface, keep fairly moist and grow in a sunny location at a night temperature of about 60° F. In mid-summer, induce dormancy by completely withholding water and setting the pot on its side in an out-of-the-way place. After 2 months of dormancy, start cycle over.

Waldsteinia

Watsonia

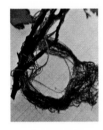

Waldsteinia ternata   Rhizome
Rosaceae, Central Europe to Siberia and Japan   Zone 4

USES: Ground Cover, Rock Garden

HABIT: Creeping evergreen plants, somewhat resembling the strawberry, with compound leaves consisting of 3 irregularly lobed leaflets, and yellow, 5-petaled flowers in spring. Plants are exceptionally low-growing, vigorous and lush.

CULTURE: Easily grown in sun or shade, having few requirements save for supplemental watering during periods of drought.

Watsonia species and hybrids   BUGLE LILY   Corm
Iridaceae, South Africa   Zone 8

USES: Garden, Cutting, Pots

HABIT: Plants have sword-shaped leaves and graceful flowering spikes up to 6 feet in height. Spikes are produced in summer and bear numerous 2-3 inch florets in white, pink, red-orange or lavender. *W. Ardernei* has white flowers; *W. bulbillifera,* which produces cormlets in the leaf axils, has orange or red blooms; *W. densiflora,* only 2-3 feet tall, has rose, or occasionally white flowers; *W. fulgens,* another 3-footer, has bright scarlet blossoms; *W. Wordsworthiana* has purple flowers.

CULTURE: In the garden, plant in the spring (fall or spring in Zones 8-10), setting 4 inches deep and 6 inches apart. Select a well-drained soil and a sunny location. Keep moist during the growing season, feeding monthly with a light application of 5-10-5. After flowering, allow to dry out, lift corms, remove dead foliage, and store in dry peat or vermiculite at 50° F.

In pots, set 5-7 corms in a 6-8 inch pot and grow in a sunny location at a night temperature of 50° F. Since plants are long-stemmed, staking will probably be necessary.

Worsleya   *Zantedeschia*

Worsleya Rayneri   BLUE AMARYLLIS   Bulb
Amaryllidaceae, Brazil

USES: Pots

HABIT: Elongated bulbs produce 18-24 inch stems bearing wavy-edged lilac-blue flowers in clusters of 8-10 during July and August. Foliage is evergreen. Grows as an epiphyte in nature.

CULTURE: Select a deep pot (12-14″), so as to provide room for 3-4 inches of drainage material such as pot shards or gravel. Fill the pot with an extremely light, well-drained mixture (coarse peat, sphagnum, or the like), planting the bulb so that only the base is in the medium. Keep fairly moist during active growth, making sure that no water contacts the foliage. Grow in full sun, maintain a 55° F. night temperature; and feed every 2 weeks with a very dilute nutrient solution. Reduce water and eliminate fertilizer during the semi-dormant period from October to December, then resume watering.

Zantedeschia species   CALLA LILY   Rhizome
Araceae, South Africa   Zone 8

USES: Garden, Pots, Cutting

HABIT: Plants with lush, arrow-shaped leaves, many attractively variegated, and fragrant, showy spathes in white, yellow, pink or maroon surrounding the prominent yellow spadix. Long-lasting in bloom. *Z. aethiopica,* the common white calla of the florists, grows to 3 feet with green leaves and white, fragrant flowers. *Z. albomaculata* grows to about 18 inches and has white-spotted foliage and spathes of white, soft yellow or pink. *Z. Elliottiana* has white-spotted leaves and bright yellow spathes. *Z. Rehmannii* has green or occasionally white-spotted leaves and rosy purple spathes.

CULTURE: In the garden, plant in a partially shaded location in a humus-enriched soil. Provide ample moisture at all times and feed generously. Rhizomes should be set 4 inches deep and 1-2 feet apart, to provide ample room for the lush, attractive foliage which is of considerable landscape value. Many will be in bloom almost constantly. In areas north of Zone 8, dig in fall, prior to frost, dry off and store in dry peat or perlite at 50° F.

In pots, select a 4-5 inch pot and cover with 3 inches of a standard potting medium. Grow at a night temperature of 60-65° F., in a fairly sunny situation, ideally shaded from direct midday sun. Keep on the dry side until growth appears, then increase water and feed regularly with soluble plant food. After flowering, gradually withhold water so leaves will wilt. Restart cycle in fall.

Zephyranthes   *Zingiber*

Zephyranthes species   ZEPHYR or RAIN LILY   Bulb
Amaryllidaceae, Subtropical America   Zone 7

USES: Border, Naturalizing, Rock Garden, Pots

HABIT: 6 to 12 inch plants with grass-like foliage and solitary upward-facing flowers in white, yellow, pink or lavender, appearing in summer and fall and often fragrant. There are many species and hybrids, the former including the often-grown *Z. candida,* white, and *Z. grandiflora,* pink.

CULTURE: In the garden, plant in fall in Zones 7-10, in spring in the North, 1-2 inches deep and 3-4 inches apart, in a well-drained soil where they will receive full sun. North of Zone 7, lift bulbs in fall and store in dry peat or perlite over winter at a temperature of 60° F.

In pots, plant 10 to a 6-inch pot, covering 2 inches deep and spacing about 1 inch apart. Use a standard potting mixture. Water thoroughly after potting, then place in a dimly-lit, cool situation until foliage appears, then transfer to a sunny location with a night temperature of 50° F. When leaves wither, withhold water for 10 weeks, then resume cycle.

Zingiber species   GINGER   Rhizome
Zingiberaceae, Tropical Asia

USES: Pots, Containers

HABIT: Plants with lanceolate leaves clasping the stems and showy inflorescens with multiple showy bracts and flowers. *Z. officinale* grows to about 2 feet and has green bracts and chartreuse flowers marked with purple and cream; the taller *Z. Zerumbet* (Bitter Ginger) has dense inflorescences with green and red bracts and yellow flowers.

CULTURE: Plant in a rich moist soil in a container large enough to permit the considerable root growth. Grow under warm conditions (night temperatures about 70° F.), under conditions of filtered light, keeping moist at all times. May be grown outdoors in shade or partial shade during warm weather.

NOTE: The root of *Z. officinale* (and other species not here mentioned) is the source of the Ginger of commerce.

PLANTS REQUIRING DRY CONDITIONS PART OR ALL OF CYCLE

Calochortus

Clivia

Ixia

Sparaxis

Sternbergia

PLANTS FOR WET OR BOGGY PLACES

Acorus

Dionaea

Iris (some species)

Sarracenia

PLANTS FOR SHADE OR PARTIAL SHADE

*Achimenes

*Aglaonema

Arisaema

Begonia

Bletilla

*Caladium

*Colocasia

Convallaria

Epimedium

Galax

*Hedychium

Hosta

*Ledebouria

Maianthemum

Mertensia

Panax

Peltiphyllum

Polemonium

Sanguinaria

*Spathiphyllum

*Denotes tender

PLANTS WITH MEDICINAL VALUE

Acorus

Colchicum

Kaempferia

Panax

Podophyllum

PLANTS OF IMPORTANT FOOD VALUE

Allium

Antigonon

Apios

Camassia

Colocasia

Crocus

Dahlia

Dioscorea

Helianthus

Hemerocallis

Ipomoea

Lilium

Pachyrrhizus

Physalis

Rheum

Solanum

Tigridia

EASY AND OUTSTANDING HOUSE PLANTS

Achimenes

Arisaema

Hippeastrum

Ledebouria

Narcissus

Neomarica

Oxalis

Sansevieria

Sinningia

Spathiphyllum

Tolmiea

Veltheimia

Zantedeschia

PLANTS FOR NATURALIZING

Anemone blanda
Asclepias
Camassia
Chionodoxa
Colchicum
Convallaria
Crocus
Endymion
Eranthis
Erythronium
Fritillaria
Galanthus
Galax
Hemerocallis
Ipheion

Leucojum
Maianthemum
Mertensia
Muscari
Narcissus
Ornithogalum
Peltiphyllum
Polemonium
Polygonatum
Sanguinaria
Scilla
Smilacina
Trillium
Uvularia

PLANTS FOR CUTTING

Acidanthera
Allium
Alstroemeria
Anemone coronaria
Convallaria
Crocosmia
Dahlia
Eremurus
Eucharis
Freesia
Galax (Foliage)
Gladiolus
Gloriosa
Iris (Bulbous types)

Kniphofia
Lilium
Lycoris
Narcissus
Nerine
Ornithogalum
Paeonia
Physalis
Polianthes
Ranunculus
Tulipa
Watsonia
Zantedeschia

BULB CHART

Sp - Spring   W - Winter   Colors   B - Blue
S - Summer   e - early   G - Green   P - Pink
F - Fall   l - late   W - White   Pu - Purple

Botanical Name	Common Name(s)	Family	Habitat	Bulb Type	N.L. of Hard Zones	Height	Colors	Bloom Period
Achimenes	Magic Flower	Gesneriaceae	Trop. Amer.	R		12-24″	Asst.	Sp,S,F
Acidanthera	Abyssinian Sword Lily	Iridaceae	Trop. and S. Africa	C	7	18-42″	W with Markings	S
Acorus	Sweet Rush	Araceae	Eur., Asia	R	3	16-24″	Y	S
Agapanthus	Lily of the Nile	Amarylli-daceae	S. Africa	R	9	18-60″	W, B	S
Aglaonema		Araceae	Trop. Asia	R		2′	W, G	
Allium, Orn.		Liliaceae	N. Hem.	B, R	4	6-60″	Asst.	Sp,S,F
Allium, Edible		Liliaceae	N. Hem.	B				Sp,S
Alocasia		Araceae	Trop. Asia	R		12-48″	G	
Alstroemeria	Peruvian Lily	Alstroe-meriaceae	S. Amer.	TR	6	24-60″	Y,O,P,R	S
Amomum		Zingiberaceae	Asia	R		2-10′	Y	
Amorpho-phallus	Devil's Tongue	Araceae	Old World Tropics	T		18-48″	R,Pu,G	
Anemone		Ranuncu-laceae	N. Temp. Zone	R	6	3-18″	Asst.	Sp,S
Anredera	Madeira Vine	Basellaceae	Trop. Amer.	TR	9	20+′	W	S
Antigonon	Coral Vine	Polygon-aceae	Trop. and Subtrop. Amer.	T	9	to 40′	P,W	S
Apios americana	Groundnut	Leguminosae	E. N. Amer. and Asia	TR	3	8′	Br	lS
Arisaema		Araceae	Medit. Reg.	T	4	18″	W,G	Sp,S
Arisarum proboscideum	Mouse Plant	Araceae	Italy	R	5	4″	Br,G	eSp

R - Red
O - Orange
Asst. - Assorted or Various

■ - Shade or Full Shade
□ - Su or Full Sun
★ - Partial or Light Shade

Uses	Sun or Shade	Planting Depth	Soil Type	Fertility	Storage	Planting Time	Comments
Pots, Hanging Baskets	★	½"-1"	Acid, Moist		70°, dry	1W,eSp	Grow warm, moist
Garden, Cutting	□	3-4"		Good+			Fragrant, resembles Gladiolus. Needs ample moisture during growth
Waterside, Pots	□		Very moist				Leaves fragrant
Pots and Patio Containers	□,★	Just covered	Porous Lime added			S	Grows best potbound
Pots	■						Attractive yellow or red berries. Tolerant of low light conditions. Grow warm and moist
Garden, Pots, Cutting		2-6"			70°, dry	Sp,F	
Food, seasoning	□			High			
Pots, Containers	■,★		Organic moist				Grow warm
Garden, Pots, Cutting	□,★	6-9"	Well-drained		50°, moist sand	Sp	Mulch in winter
Pots, Containers	★		Moist	Fertile			Leaves aromatic. Grow warm
Pots, Containers	★		Moist			Sp	Dormant in winter. Grow warm
Garden, Cutting	□,★	2-3"			70°, dry		
Containers, Trellis, Screen (where hardy)	□	3-4"				Sp	Fragrant vine
Garden Screen (where hardy) Containers	□		Moist				Edible Tubers
Wild Garden							Fragrant flowers. Edible tubers
Pots	□,★	4"		Fertile			Colorful berries
Ground cover	★		Moist				Dormant in summer

147

Asarum	Wild Ginger	Aristolo-chiaceae	N. Temp. Zone	R	4	6"	Br	Sp
Asclepias tuberosa	Butterfly Weed	Asclepi-adaceae	U. S.	TR	3	2-3'	O,R,Y	S
Begonia x tuberhybrida	Tuberous Begonia	Begoniaceae	From Andean Species	T		12-18"	Asst. No B,Pu	S
Begonia grandis		Begoniaceae	Asia	T	6	2-3'	P,W,	
Belamcanda	Blackberry Lily	Iridaceae	China and Japan	R	5	30-36"	R,O,Y	S
Bletilla striata		Orchidaceae	Temp. E. Asia	R	5	12-24"	W,P,Pu	S
Bowiea volubilis	Climbing Onion	Liliaceae	Trop. and S. Africa	B		5-15'	G,W	
Brodiaea		Amarylli-daceae	W. North America	C	7	12-36"	R,Y,B, W,Pu	Sp,eS
Caladium x hortulanum		Araceae	Trop. Amer.	T		18"	Asst. Leaves	
Calathea		Marantaceae	Trop. Amer.	T		6-60"	W,Y,Pu	
Calochortus, Mariposa		Liliaceae	W. North America	B	5	6-48"	Asst.	Sp
Camassia		Liliceae	N. Amer.	B	3	18-36"	B,W	Sp
Canna		Cannaceae	Trop. and Subtrop.	T,R	7	18-60"	W,Y,O, P,R	S
Chionodoxa	Glory-of-the-Snow	Lilaceae	Asia Minor & Greek Islands	B	3	6-10"	W,P,B	eSp
Claytonia	Spring Beauty	Portu-lacaceae	N. Amer.	B	6	4-12"	P,W	eSp
Clivia		Amarylli-daceae	S. Africa	TR	10	18-24"	R,Y,O, P,W	
Colchicum		Liliaceae	Eur., N. Afr. W. & C. Asia	C	4	6-12"	W,P, Pu,Y	F,Sp
Colocasia	Elephant's Ear Taro, Dasheen	Araceae	Trop. Asia	C	10	4-6'	G,Pu	S

Use		Depth	Soil	Temp	Season	Remarks
Ground cover	★		Moist			Requires ample moisture
Garden, Naturalizing	□		Very well-drained	Low		Large clumps difficult to move. Slow to break dormancy.
Garden, Pots, Baskets	★		Peaty	45°, in dry peat	Sp	
Garden, Wild Garden	★		Humsy		Sp	Fragrant
Garden, Dried Arrangements	□,★	4″			Sp,F	
Garden, Pot Cutting	★	4″	Moist, Organic	36°,	Sp,F	Dormant fall and winter
Pots	★	P. above ground				Rest summer and fall
Garden, Pots	□	4″			F	Grow moist, no manure
Garden, Pots	★	1″		70°, dry	Sp	Grown for foliage, syringe foliage when hot, start with bottom heat.
Pots	★		Moist, porous humusy	Fertile		Attractive variegated leaves, some tubers edible, grow warm
Garden	★	2″	Gritty		F	Grow dry in summer
Gardens, Naturalizing	□,★	3-4″	Moist	70°, dry		Bulbs edible. Grow warm
Gardens, Containers	□	1-2″		60°, moist	Sp	Some have bronze leaves, 1 species edible tuber, likes heat
Garden Naturalizing	□,★	3″	Ex-good drainage	70°, dry	F	Best in mass plantings
Wild Garden						
Pots and Patio Containers	★	Barely covered	Heavy			Fragrant, grow dry W, S, Sp. Best potbound
Garden, Forcing	□,★	3-4″	Rich, gritty with humus		eS	Leaves in spring only, can force unplanted
Garden, Container	□,★	4″	Peaty		Sp	Edible, source of Poi, high humidity

Convallaria majalis		Liliaceae	Temp. N. Hemis.	R	3-7	8"	W,P	Sp
Costus	Spiral Flag	Zingiber-aceae	Pantropics	R		1-10'	Y,O,R,W	
Corydalis		Fumariaceae	N. Temp. Zone	R,T	5	6-18"	P,Y	Sp,S
Crocosmia	Montebretia	Iridaceae	S. Africa	C	6	2-4'	Y,O,R	S,F
Crocus		Iridaceae	Medit. Reg. & Asia Minor	C	3	2-6"	Asst. No R	Sp,F
Cyclamen		Primulaceae	Medit, C. Eur. Asia Minor	T	5-9	6-15"	W,P,R	Sp,F
Dahlia		Compositae	Mexico and C. Amer.	TR		1-7'	Asst. No B	S,F
Dicentra		Fumariaceae	N. Amer. and Asia	T,R	4	1-3'	P,W	Sp,S
Dichelostemma		Amarylli-daceae	W. North America	C	4	1-3'	R,Pu,P	
Dietes vegeta		Iridaceae	Trop. and S. Africa	R	9	2-4'	W,Y,B, Y,Br,W	
Dionaea muscipula	Venus Fly Trap	Droseraceae	The Carolinas	R	8	6-12"	W	S
Dioscorea		Diosco-reaceae	Warmer Reg. W. World	TR				
Disporum	Fairy-Bells	Liliaceae	N. Amer. and Asia	R	4	2-2½'	W,Y	Sp,S
Dracunculus		Araceae	Old World	T	8	18		
Endymion hispanicus	Scilla campanu-lata, Wood Hyacinth	Liliaceae	W. Eur. and N. W. Africa	B	4	12-20"	W,P,B	eSp
Epimedium		Berberi-daceae	Temp. Eur. and Asia	R	5	6-18"	W,P, R,Pu	eSp, eS

Use		Depth	Soil	Temperature	Season	Notes
Gardens, Ground Cover, Pots, Cutting	★,■	1″	Acid, moist	36°, moist	F,Sp	Apply organic fertilizer
Containers	■,★		Moist			
Garden	■,★		Well-drained	70°, dry		
Garden, Cutting	□	2″	Well-drained		Sp	
Gardens, Naturalizing	□,★	1-2″	Very low		eS,F	Best in cool areas
Garden, Cutting	□		Well-drained	50°, dry	Sp	
Garden, Cutting	□	6″, but fill in gradually	Organic	60° dry or in sawdust	Sp	Edible. Stake at planting time
Garden, Naturalizing	□,■				Sp,F	
Pots, Garden (where hardy)						
Pots, Terrarium	□		Sphagnum			Requires constant moisture
						Several species edible, vines
Wild Garden						
Pots	□	6″ in garden	good drainage			Carrion odor, scarlet berries
Garden, Naturalizing	□,★	3-4″	Moist, highly organic		F	Colonizes rapidly
Ground Cover, Edging, Rock Garden	★			Low	Sp,F	Supply ample moisture

Eranthis	Winter Aconite	Ranuncu-laceae	Eur. and Asia	T	4	2-4"	Y	eW, eSp
Eremurus	Desert Candle	Liliaceae	W & C Asia	TR	5-9	3-9'	W,P,Y,O	S
Erythronium	Trout Lily, Dog-Tooth's Violet	Liliaceae	Temp. N. Amer. Eur. and Asia	C	3-9	6-24"	Y,P,Pu	Sp
Eucharis		Amarylli-daceae	C. and S. America	B		12-24"	W	lW, eS
Eucomis	Pineapple Lily	Liliaceae	S. Africa	B	7	12-24'	W,P	S
Ferraria		Iridaceae	S. Africa	C		1½'	P,Y	Sp,eS
Freesia		Iridaceae	S. Africa	C	9	12-18"	Asst.	Sp
Fritillaria	Crown Imperial, Guinea Hen Flower	Liliaceae	Eur. and Asia	B	3-5	12" 2½-4'	Pu,R, O,Y	Sp
Galanthus	Snowdrop	Amarylli-daceae	Eur. and Asia	B	3-9	4-9"	W	eSp
Galax urceolata		Diapen-siaceae	E. Amer.	R	4	1"	W	lS
Geranium tuberosum		Geraniaceae	S. Eur.	T	6	12-15"	Pu	S
Gladiolus		Iridaceae	Medit. Reg. & S. Africa	C	8	1-5"	Asst.	S
Gloriosa		Liliaceae	Africa and Asia	T		3-6'	Y,R	S
Gloxinia		Gesneriaceae	C. and S. America	R		12-30"	B,Pu, P,W	
Habranthus		Amarylli-daceae	The Americas	B	9	6-12"	P,Y	S
Haemanthus		Amarylli-daceae	Africa	B		8-24"	R,P,W	Sp,S

Use		Depth	Soil	Temperature	Season	Notes
Garden	□, ★	2-3″	Moist	70°, dry	eF	Soak in water 24 hours hours before planting
Garden, Cutting	□	6″		70°, dry	F	Foliage dies back in summer. Likes heat, do not disturb. Moist during growing season.
Gardens, Naturalizing	★	2-3″	Moist	45°, moist	F	Slightly fragrant, tolerant of heat and drought. Best cool.
Pots, Cutting Containers	★	Flush with surface	Moist	70°, dry	F	Fragrant, best potbound Grow warm and moist, induce dormancy
Pots, Containers	□	5-6″ just covered in pots		45°, dry	eSp	Spotted foliage. Grow dry in winter, moist during growth
Pots	□		Humusy			Dry off when foliage dies
Pots, Cutting	□			70°, dry		May require staking, grow cool.
Garden	□	3-4″/6″	Very well-drained	70°, dry	eS,eF	Bulbs and plants of F. imp. have musky odor. F. imperialis requires excellent drainage
Garden		2-3″			F	Culture varies with species. Best cool.
Naturalizing, Cutting (foliage)	★		Lime-free			Cool woodlands
Garden						
Garden, Cutting	□	6″	Light	45°, dry	Sp	Outstanding cut flowers. No Manure!
Garden Vine, Pots, Cutting	□	4-5″		60°, dry	Sp	
Pots	★		Moist humusy			Grow warm and humid
Rock Garden,		2-3″ pots 4-6″ gar.	Sandy	60°, dry	Sp	
Containers, Pots	□	Tip just above surface		50° in pot	eW, eSp	Keep dry until growth starts, induce dormancy

Hedychium		Zingiber-aceare	Trop. Asia and Himal.	R	10	4-7'	W,Y,R	S
Helianthus tuberosus	Jersusalem Artichoke	Compositae	The Americas	T	5	12'	Y	lS
Helleborus		Ranuncu-laceae	Eur. and Asia	TR	3	1-3'	W,R,Pu,G	lW,eSp
Hemerocallis		Liliaceae	C. Eur., China, and Japan	TR	4	1½-3'	Y,O,P,R,Pu	eSp,lS
Hermodactylus tuberosus	Snake's Head Iris	Iridaceae	Medit. Reg.	T	6	12"	Pu,G	Sp
Hippeastrum hybrids		Amarylli-daceae	S. Amer.	B	9	12-24"	R,O,P,W	W,Sp
Hippeastrum species		Amarylli-daceae	S. Amer.		B		1-4'	W,Y,G,P
Homeria	Cape Tulip	Iridaceae	S. Africa	C	10	12-18"	Y,R,Pu	Sp,eS
Hosta	Plantain Lily, Funkia	Liliaceae	Japan, China, Korea	R	3	1-5'	W,Pu	S,F
Hyacinthus	Hyacinth	Liliaceae	Medit. and Asia Minor	B	4	9-18"	Asst.	Sp
Hymenocallis	Ismene Peruvian Daffodil	Amarylli-daceae	N. and S. Amer.	B	8	18-24"	W,Y	S
Incarvillea	Hardy Gloxinia	Bignoniaceae	China	TR	6	24"	Pu	eSp,eS
Ipheion		Amarylli-daceae	S. Amer.	B		6"	B,W	Sp
Ipomoea	Sweet Potato	Convolvu-laceae	Pantropics	TR	8		P	S
Iris		Iridaceae		B,R				Sp
Ixia		Iridaceae	S. Africa	C	9	18"	R,P,Y,O	eSp,eS
Ixiolirion	Lily of the Altai	Amarylli-daceae	Asia	B	7	12-16"	B	eSp,eS
Kaempferia		Zingiber-aceae	Asia and Africa	R				
Kniphofia	Red Hot Poker Tritoma	Liliaceae	Trop. and S. Africa	R	5	1-3'	Y,O	

Garden, Pots	★	1″	Moist	Fertile		Sp	Many fragrant. Ample water all times. Induce dormancy in fall.
Food Crop	□		Well-drained				Edible tubers
Garden	□,★		Well-drained moist				Evergreen, toxic. prefers lime
Garden Naturalizing	□,★						Among the easiest
Garden	□		Well-drained				
Garden, Pots	□	2-3″ gar. ½ above soil in pot			45°, dry	F,W	Grow on in summer, then induce dormancy
Pots	□					F	Grow cool, start dark
Border, Edging	□,■		Moist	High		Sp,F	Water during drought
Garden, Pots							Very fragrant
Garden, Pots	□,★	3-5″	Well-drained, humusy		70°, dry	Sp	Fragrant
Garden, Rock Garden	□	2″	Rich, acid	High		Sp	Blooms prior to foliage. Keep moist during growth, remove faded flowers
Garden, Pots, Naturalizing	□	3″	Well-drained			F	Colonize rapidly. Winter mulch
Garden, Pots, Rock Garden, Cutting							Varies with species
Garden, Pots		3″	Extra good drainage			lF	Grow dry
Cutting							
Garden, Cutting	□	3″		Very low!		F,Sp	
							Some species used for medicine, flavoring
Garden	□					Sp,F	Require excellent drainage. Remove spent flowers

Koellikeria		Gesneriaceae	Cent. and S. Amer.	R		12″	Pu	S
Ledebouria		Liliaceae	S. Africa	B	9	8″	G,Pu	eSp
Leontopodium alpinum	Edelweiss	Compositae	Europe and Asia	R	5	6″	W,Y	S
Leucojum	Snowflake	Amaryllidaceae	Europe	B	4	6-12″	W	eSp, eS
Lewisia		Portulacaceae	Western N. Amer.	TR,C	5	2-12″	W,P,R	Sp
Liatris		Compositae	N. Amer.	C,R	3	3-5′	Pu,W	S,F
Lilium	Lily	Liliaceae	N. Temp. Zone	B	3		Asst. No B	
Lycoris	Magic or Resurrection Lily, Spider Lily	Amaryllidaceae	China, Japan, and Burma	B	5-8		P,R, W,Y	S
Maianthemum		Liliaceae	Canada and Adj. U. S. A.	R	3	8″	W	Sp
Maranta	Prayer Plant	Marantaceae	Trop. Amer.	T,R		6-18″	W,P	Sp
Mertensia	Virginia Bluebell	Boraginaceae	Asia, Europe, E. N. Amer.	TR	4	1-3′	B,P	Sp
Milla		Amaryllidaceae	U. S. A., Mexico and C. Amer.	C	8	6-20″	W	S,F
Mirabilis Jalapa	Four O'Clock Marvel of Peru	Nyctaginaceae		TR		2-3′	W,Y,R	S
Muscari	Grape, Plume Hyacinth	Liliaceae	Medit. and S. W. Asia	B	2	6-12″	B,W, P,Pu	Sp
Narcissus	Daffodil	Amaryllidaceae	S. Europe and N. Africa	B	4-8	6-24″	W,Y	eSp, Sp
Neomarica	Apostle Plant Walking Iris	Iridaceae	Cent. and S. Amer.	R	10	12-24″	W,Br, W,B	
Nerine		Amaryllidaceae	S. Africa	B	9	8-18″	P,R,W	eS,F

Use		Depth	Soil		Temp	Season	Comments
Pots	★		Moist, humusy				
Pots	★	Partially above soil					Mottled foliage
Rock Garden	□		Dry				
Garden, Naturalizing	□,★	3-4″				eF	
Rock Garden							Some species have edible roots. Ample spring moisture, hot and dry rest of year
	□		Well-drained	Low			Trim off spent flowers
Garden, Cutting, Pots	□,★	1-8″	Extra good drainage			lS,lF,Sp, some available late	Grow with shade at roots in sun. L. candidium needs early, shallow planting
Garden, Pots	□,★	3-5″			45°, dry	eS,F,Sp	Foliage of L. squamigera dies before flowering.
Ground Cover, Naturalizing	■		Moist, acid humusy			Sp,F	Fragrant
Pots	■		Moist				Constant moisture during growth. Grow drier in winter. Handsome colored leaves. 1 species source of arrow-root for cooking.
Garden, Naturalizing	★	2″	Rich, moist humusy			F	Foliage dies in June
Garden, Pots	□	3″	Extra good drainage				Fragrant
							Fragrant, open late afternoon.
Garden, Rock Garden, Naturalizing	□,★	3″			70°, dry	eF	Fragrant
Garden, Pots, Naturalizing	□,★	5-9″				eF	
Pots	□						Extra-easy house plant
Pots, Cutting		3-6″				S,eF	Best potbound, do not disturb

157

Ophiopogon	Lily Turf, Mondo Grass	Liliaceae	India and Korea	R		6-24"		
Orchis		Orchidaceae	N. Amer.	R	4	1-2'	P,Pu	eS
Ornithogalum		Liliaceae	Africa, Europe and W. Asia	B			W,Y	Sp
Oxalis		Oxalidaceae	S. Africa and S. Amer.	B,T,R	7	4-12"	P,R, Y,W	
Pachyrhizus tuberosus	Yam Bean	Leguminosae	Trop. Amer.	TR				
Paeonia		Paeoniaceae	China, Tibet, and Siberia	R	3	2-4"	P,R,W	Sp
Panax	Ginseng	Araliaceae	N. Amer. and E. Asia	R	3	12-24"	W	eS
X Pardancanda		Iridaceae		R	5	30-60"	Asst.	S
x Paschia		Gesneriaceae					Pu	
Pecteilis	Heron Flower	Orchidaceae	Japan	T		24"	W	eS
Peltiphyllum		Saxifragaceae	Pac. N. W.	R	5	12"	P	eSp
Physalis		Solanaceae	The Americas	R	3			
Pleione		Orchidaceae	India, China, Thailand, and Taiwan	C			W,P	
Podophyllum	Mayapple	Berberi- daceae	N. Amer. and Asia	R	3	1'	W,P,Pu	Sp
Polemonium	Jacob's Ladder	Polemoni- aceae	Europe, Asia, and The Amer.	R	3	1-3'	P,Y,Pu	eSp, eS
Polianthes	Tuberose	Agavaceae	Mexico	R		1-4'	W	S
Polygonatum	Solomon's Seal	Liliaceae	N. Amer., Europe and and Asia	R	4	2½'	W	eSp, eS
Puschkinia	Striped Squill	Liliaceae	Asia Minor	B	3-9	4-8"	B&W,W	Sp
Ranunculus	Buttercup	Ranuncu- laceae	Europe	TR	8	18"	Asst. No B	eSp
Rheum	Rhubarb	Polygon- aceae			3	2-3'	W,R	

Ground Cover, Garden edging, Pots	★		Moist			Sp	
	□	3"	Humusy			lS,eF	
Garden, Pots, Cutting	□,★	2-3"				F	O. thyrsoides is outstanding cut flower
Pots	□	2"			60°, dry	F,S	Grow moist
							Some species edible
Garden, Cutting	□,★ in South	1"	Extra good			lS,eF	Fragrant. An especially long-lived plant
Naturalizing	■	2"	Organic			F,Sp	Will not tolerate sun. Alleged medicinal use.
Pots	★		Moist				
Pots	□	Just covered	Well-drained		40°, dry	eW,eSp	Foliage marked silver. Grow like Sinningia
Border, Water-side, naturalizing	■,★		Moist				Very lush foliage Grow cool.
							Some with edible fruit.
Wild Garden			Moist humusy				Spreads rapidly. Fruits edible, drug from rhizome
Garden	□,★					Sp	
Garden, Cutting	□	3"			60°, dry	eSp	Very fragrant, grow warm
Garden, Naturalizing	■,★		Acid, Organic	High		F,Sp	Do not disturb
Garden, Rock Garden	□,★	2-3"	Sandy			F	
Garden, Cutting	□	1½"			60°, dry	Sp,F	Outstanding for cutting. Soak overnight in water prior to planting. Likes cool nights.
Food Plant	□,★		Moist	Fertile		Sp,F	Grow cool

Rhodohypoxis		Hypoxi-daceae	S. Africa	R		6″	P	
Sanguinaria canadensis	Bloodroot	Papaveraceae	E. North America	R	3	8″	W	Sp
Sansevieria		Agavaceae	Africa and S. Asia	R		6-48″	W	
Sarracenia	Pitcher Plant	Sarraceni-aceae	The Americas	R	5	1′	Pu,R,Y	eS
Scilla		Liliaceae	Africa, Europe, and Asia	B			B,P,W	Sp
Sinningia speciosa	Gloxinia	Gesneriaceae	Mexico, C. and S. Amer.	T,R		8-12″	Asst.	Sp,S
Sinningia cardinalis		Gesneriaceae	Brazil	R		8-12″	R	Sp,S
Smilacina	False Solomon's Seal	Liliaceae	N. Amer. and Asia	R	4	18-30″	W	eSp
Smithiantha	Temple Bells	Gesneriaceae	Mexico	R		9-18″	R,O,Y,W	Sp,S
Solanum tuberosum	Potato	Solanaceae	Andes	T	3	3′	W,B	S
Spathiphyllum		Araceae	Trop. Amer.	R		1-3′	W,Y,G	
Sparaxis	Harlequin Flower	Iridaceae	S. Africa	C		12-18″	Asst.	Sp
Spathicarpa		Araceae	S. Amer.	T,R			G	
Sprekelia formosissima	Jacobean Lily	Amarylli-daceae	Mexico	B	8	12-18″	R	S Sp pot
Sternbergia lutea		Amarylli-daceae	S. E. Europe	B	6	6-9″	Y	F
Streptanthera		Iridaceae	S. Africa	C		6-12″	O	Sp

	□, ★				F,Sp	Plants go dormant S,F, W. Summer mulch, provide ample moisture.
Pots						Fragrant; low light tolerant; easy.
Bog Planting, Terrarium			sphagnum Peat			Constant moisture
Garden, Rock Garden, Naturalizing, some are pot subjects only		2-3″				Leaves of hardy species die in early summer.
Pots	★	1″	Peaty	70°, peat	lW,eS	Outstanding pot plant, grow warm.
Woodland Planting	■		Lime-free			Fragrant, aggressive
Pots	★		Moist			Handsome velvety, often colored leaves. Grow like Sinningia.
Food Plant	□	2-3″		Very high	eSp	Grow at pH 5.4 or below to prevent scab.
Pots	★,■		Moist			Excellent house plants, low-light tolerant.
Garden, Rock Gardens, Cutting Pots	□	2-3″				Requires dry summers
Pots	★		Moist			
Garden, Pots	□	3-4″ with neck protruding in pots			S,W pots	Performs best in garden when allowed to dry out and become crowded
Garden, Rock Garden		5″	dry, gritty	Low	lS	Failure to flower usually because of too much moisture
Pots	□		Moist		Sp	

Symphytum	Comfrey	Boraginaceae	Europe and W. Asia	TR	4	6-18"	Asst.	S
Synnotia		Iridaceae	S. Africa	C				
Tacca	Bat Plant	Taccaceae	Asia	R			R,Pu	eW,Sp
Talinum paniculatum	Jewels of Opar	Portulacaceae	S. U. S. A. C. Amer.	TR	7	2½'	R,Y	S
Tecophilaea		Tecophilaeaceae	Chilean Andes	C				
Tigridia		Iridaceae	Mexico, Cent. N. South Amer.	B	7	18-30"	Asst., No B or Pu	S
Tolmiea Menziesii	Piggyback Plant	Saxifragaceae	W. N. Amer.	R	6	2'	G,W	
Trillium	Wake Robin	Liliaceae	N. Amer., Himalayas and E. Asia	TR	3	12-48"	W,P, R,Pu	Sp
Triteleia		Amaryllidaceae	W. N. Amer.	C				
Tulbaghia violacea	Society Garlic	Amaryllidaceae	Trop. and S. Africa	T,C	9	1-2½'	Pu,P	F,W, Sp
Tulipa	Tulip	Liliaceae	Cent. Asia and Asia Minor	B	3-7	3-30"	Asst. No B	
Uvularia		Liliaceae	E. N. Amer.	R	3	12-18"	Y	Sp,eS
Vallota speciosa	Scarborough Lily	Amaryllidaceae	S. Africa	B	9	24"	R,P,W	eS,F
Veltheimia		Liliaceae	S. Africa	B	9	18"	Y,P	eW
Waldsteinia		Rosaceae	N. Hemisphere	R	4	4"	Y	Sp
Watsonia		Iridaceae	S. Africa	C	8	2½-6'	R,P,O,W	S
Worsleya Rayneri	Blue Amaryllis	Amaryllidaceae	Brazil	B		18-24"	B	
Zantedeschia		Araceae	S. Africa	R	8	1½-4'	W,P,Y	Sp,eS
Zephyranthes		Amaryllidaceae	Subtropical W. Hemisphere	B	7	6-12"	W,Y, P,Pu	S,eF
Zingiber		Zingiberaceae	Trop. Asia	R,TR		18-24"	G,R,Y	lS

Use	Light	Depth	Soil/Moisture	Temp.	Season	Notes
Ground Cover, Garden	□, ★		Moist		F,Sp	Leave undisturbed
Pots	★		Moist		F,W	
Garden	□	4″	Extra good drainage	60°, dry	Sp	Edible bulb, tastes like chestnuts. Grow like Gladiolus
Baskets, Pots, Ground cover	★		Moist			Easy house plant, new plants from adventitious leaves
Garden, Naturalizing	★		Well-drained humusy		Sp,F	Do not cut leaves, keep moist
Garden, Pots	□	Tips at surface	Moist, humusy			Any time Fragrant
Garden, Rock Gardens, Cutting	□	3-8″			F	Deep plantings may prolong life
Naturalizing	★,■		Well-drained Organic		F,Sp	
Garden, Pots	□	Tip just covered	Well-drained		S,F	
Pots	★	½ bulb exposed			lS,eF	
Rock Garden, Ground Cover	□,■					Water during drought
Garden, Cutting	□	4″		50° peat	W	Grow moist during active growth
Pots		Only base covered	Very well-drained			No water on foliage, dormant Oct.-Dec.
Garden, Pots, Cutting	★	3-4″	Moist	45°, dry	Sp	Grow constantly moist. Some with spotted foliage
Border, Rock Garden, Pots, Naturalizing	□	2″	Well-drained		Sp	
Pots, Containers	★		Moist			

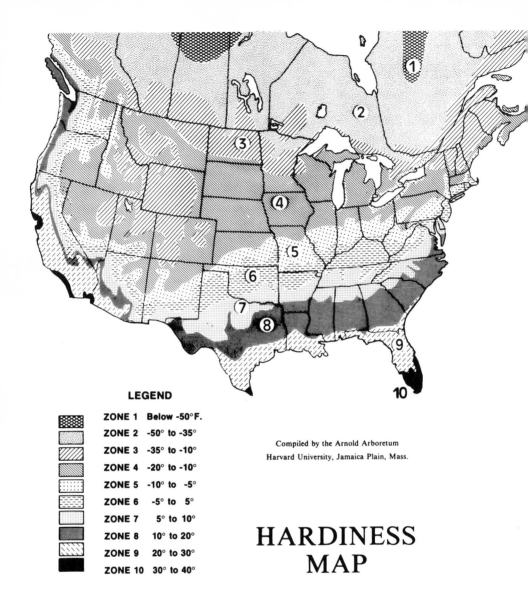

LEGEND

	ZONE 1	Below -50°F.
	ZONE 2	-50° to -35°
	ZONE 3	-35° to -10°
	ZONE 4	-20° to -10°
	ZONE 5	-10° to -5°
	ZONE 6	-5° to 5°
	ZONE 7	5° to 10°
	ZONE 8	10° to 20°
	ZONE 9	20° to 30°
	ZONE 10	30° to 40°

Compiled by the Arnold Arboretum
Harvard University, Jamaica Plain, Mass.

HARDINESS MAP

The above hardiness map was developed by the Arnold Arboretum, Harvard University, Jamaica Plain, Mass., and is reproduced through their courtesy. The hardiness zones 1-10 are based on the average annual minimum temperatures for each zone and divide the United States and Canada into areas where specific plants perform best as to winter hardiness. Many factors, such as altitude, degree of exposure to wind, modifying effect of bodies of water, soil types and the like can create variations of as much as two zones within a geographical area, but adhering to your specific zone will generally give you the best results. Often, however, inhabitants of the southernmost portion of one zone can safely use plants for the next, more northerly zone.

CROSS REFERENCE INDEX

Listed here are the botanical and common names of the plants described in this book. Included under common names are commonly mis-applied botanical names, and those used with other genera.

Plant nomenclature in this book is based on *Hortus III.*